# Zoo Doctor

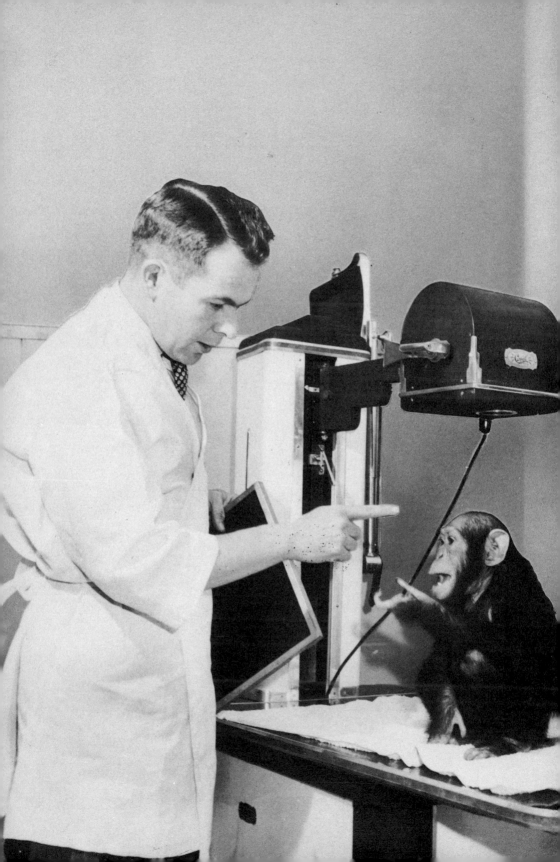

# ZOO
# DOCTOR

### By WILLIAM BRIDGES
Curator of Publications
New York Zoological Park

WILLIAM MORROW & COMPANY
New York                                    1957

Library of Congress Catalog Card Number: 56-8482

. . . .

For Michael,
a happy and fortunate boy
whose father is the zoo doctor
of these stories.

# Contents

# Foreword

The veterinarian of New York's great Bronx Zoo often gets letters from young people who want to know how to become a zoo doctor. Sometimes they come to the Animal Hospital and have serious talks with the doctor about training for a career in veterinary medicine.

The stories in *Zoo Doctor* are a kind of supplement to these talks; they are examples of the daily problems in the life of a busy zoo doctor. They show the satisfaction the doctor gets from work that in a way repays animals for the pleasure they give to millions of zoo visitors.

The photographs are the work of Sam Dunton, F.B.P.A., the Bronx Zoo's skilled staff photographer, except for those in the chapter "Lions in the Living Room," which were taken by Arthur Sasse, of International News Photos.

W. B.

# The Zoo Doctor

The first man to arrive at the Bronx Zoo's Animal Hospital one summer morning was Jim, the hospital attendant. Jim hoped to be a keeper in one of the zoo's animal buildings some day, and he rather had his eye on a job in the Monkey House, for most of the animals that lived there were small and friendly. He always tried to make friends with the zoo animals, and he had found that almost any monkey would become a pet if he talked to it and played with it long enough.

It was just eight o'clock when he arrived, a whole hour before the doctor and the nurse were due. Jim always came to work early, so he could get the cleaning and feeding of the animal patients out of the way before the real work of the day started. This morning the usual chorus of screeches and howls greeted him as he unlocked the door. Keechee, the little olive baboon, was always the first to hear him, because she lived in a cage that opened off the hallway just inside the front door. Keechee wasn't sick; she lived in the Animal Hospital simply because there was no room for her anywhere else. Jim talked to her just the way he would have spoken to a child, and Keechee generally talked back just as a very badly spoiled human child would have done—only she talked in baboon language. Her yells, screeches, and screams sounded as if she were having a temper tantrum, but all they really meant was that Keechee was glad to see her friend.

"Keechee, I've got a notion to tell the doctor that you don't know how to behave," Jim scolded. "Look what you've done to the floor!" During the night Keechee had thrown out all the food she didn't want to eat, and the hallway was littered with pieces of carrot, apple, orange, banana, lettuce, cabbage, and grapes. "I'll have to work all morning cleaning up the mess you've made."

Keechee didn't seem to mind Jim's scolding, especially since he ended it by fishing in his coat pocket and bringing out a paper-wrapped lump of sugar for her. She snatched it out of his hand and in one leap sprang up on the shelf at the back of her compartment. There, with her little brown eyes intent on the sugar and her eyebrows twitching up and down as she frowned in concentration, she picked the paper off the lump of sugar and popped the sugar into her mouth.

Jim turned away. The day was starting normally, but there was no time to waste in playing with Keechee. He hurried to the dressing room at the end of the hall and changed from his street clothes into the khaki pants and shirt he wore while on duty in the hospital.

His first job was to make the rounds of the hospital cages and see whether each one of the patients had come through the night all right. Pop, the hyacinthine macaw, squawked a greeting and waddled to the front of his cage as Jim entered the ward. Pop was a sight; his head was as bald as an egg, and his back was covered with ragged patches of dark and light blue feathers, as if moths had been at work on him. He was having trouble molting (dropping out his old feathers and growing new ones), but he was getting along all right. Jim noticed with satisfaction that he had eaten most of the sunflower seeds in the pan that had been placed in his cage the night before.

The South American kinkajou was about the same as yesterday; he hadn't eaten much of his fruit and chopped meat. The little honey-colored animal was not feeling very well. He lay half curled up on a bed of hay and merely looked up when Jim stood in front of him. His trouble was internal parasites, which kinkajous often have, but Jim was not worried. The doctor would get him to swallow a good dose of a kind of medicine that would destroy the parasites, and in a few days he would be climbing all over the cage and wanting to be petted.

The two young harbor seals from Maine were the only problem at the moment. They had arrived only yesterday afternoon and were such babies that they didn't know how to eat fish yet, or how to drink milk from a nursing bottle. The doctor was going to have a hard time teaching them to feed. Or, rather, Jim was going to have a hard time, for he was pretty sure the doctor would go through the feeding once, while he himself looked on, and then say, "Well, Jim, that's how to do it. From now on you feed the babies twice a day."

Fortunately, there weren't many patients in the Animal Hospital right now. There was a big pileated woodpecker that someone had found along the road, with a broken wing. The doctor had already cleaned the injured wing and taken out bits of shattered bone. The woodpecker could never fly again; but it would be able to hop and climb, and hammer with its powerful beak. It would always have plenty to eat in the zoo and it would probably live even longer than it normally would have lived in the wild.

The only other patient was a shy, nervous agile wallaby, one of the smallest of the kangaroos from Australia. It was a newcomer to the zoo's animal collection, and the doctor wanted to keep it in the hospital for about a week and examine it for parasites and contagious diseases before it joined the other kangaroos in the Kangaroo House. There didn't seem to be anything the matter with it, for it was eating all its cut-up vegetables and grain. It was just in quarantine until the doctor could be sure it was as healthy as it looked.

As Jim made the rounds of the cages, he took out the feeding trays from the night before and removed the watering dishes, scrubbing each one at the sink in the hospital's kitchen before filling it with fresh water and replacing it. Pop, the macaw, got a fresh dish of seeds, because birds like to eat at odd times all through the day. The wallaby wouldn't get another meal until midmorning, and he would get his next one late in the afternoon. Jim prepared a small dish of ground meat and hard-boiled egg for the pileated woodpecker. Keechee didn't need anything more (she would only waste it), and the kinkajou and the harbor seals were problems for the doctor to figure out.

Jim finished the morning feeding, then swept out the cages and hosed them down. When he turned the hose on the floor of Keechee's compartment, she always screamed her head off and fled to the highest shelf to get out of the way of the water. She wasn't really afraid of it, though. Once when Jim was called to the telephone and left the hose running within reach of Keechee's eager fingers, she pulled it into the cage and turned it on him when he came back to finish the job!

Jim had just finished calling the cook room to order the

day's supplies of fruits and vegetables and fish and meat for the patients when the telephone on the doctor's desk rang. It was the bear keeper.

"Tell the doc to take a look at that black bear, will you, Jim? He's got a running nose."

"O.K., I'll tell him."

Jim was used to all sorts of telephone calls from the keepers early in the morning. They always made the same kind of inspection of their animals as he did, looking at each one closely to see whether it had eaten well, or had developed an illness overnight. If the slightest trouble showed up, they always telephoned the hospital to report to Jim, who would pass the information on to the doctor.

It was just a few minutes before nine o'clock when the doctor arrived. Although he was still a young man when he had become the zoo's veterinarian, or animal doctor, he had a good many years of special training behind him. It had started when he was still in grade school. He had kept dogs and cats, and a pet raccoon, and garter snakes, and a tame crow at home; and even if they didn't have anything the matter with them, he was always reading about the diseases of animals and planning what he would do for his pets if they ever got sick.

Long before he was ready to go to college, he had made up his mind he was going to be a veterinarian and specialize in the diseases and treatment of wild animals. All through high school he planned his courses with veterinary medicine in mind. He studied three foreign languages so that he could read scientific papers in them, as well as in English, and he took all the courses in zoology, physiology, genetics, compara-

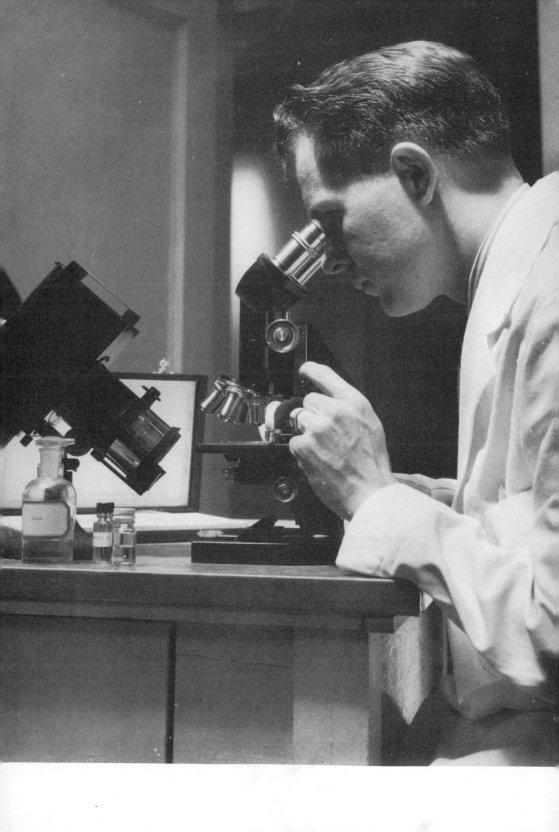

tive pathology, and comparative anatomy that he could crowd into his school schedules. He was first in his class when he was graduated from the veterinary school of one of the great state universities in the Midwest, with the degree of D.V.M. —Doctor of Veterinary Medicine. Plenty of jobs were waiting for him. For five years he did research on animal diseases. Then the Bronx Zoo needed a veterinarian to replace its animal doctor, who had gone to another zoo, and his life's ambition was realized. He was going to be a zoo doctor and put his years of training and knowledge at the service of wild animals.

"Everything quiet, I hope," the doctor said to Jim, as he entered his office in the Animal Hospital.

"There are only one or two things. The kinkajou didn't eat much of anything last night, and the bear keeper called up and said the black bear has a running nose."

"That isn't much. Don't feed the kinkajou this morning, and I'll put some medication in his afternoon meal. I'll look in on the black bear while I'm making rounds this morning."

Like Jim, the doctor made a quick tour of inspection of the patients in the hospital. All of them were doing reasonably well, and there was nothing to worry about—except the two little harbor seals. They *had* to be taught how to eat.

Jim's early-morning cleaning work was about over, and he and the doctor put on the short-sleeved white hospital gowns they wore over their regular clothes while they were handling the animals. They had just finished when the nurse came in. She had changed from street clothes to her white uniform and was ready for work. She, too, was specially qualified for her job. She had received her training in a New York City hospital, and was entitled to write R.N. (Registered Nurse) after her name. Because of her training she was able to take care of any small injury, such as a cut or a splinter in the finger, that might happen to zoo employees or to visitors. She could also handle the dozens of special jobs that occurred in the Animal Hospital.

This morning she had plenty to do, for the doctor had told her the night before that he wanted a dozen agar slants prepared in test tubes, in readiness for some bacterial cultures he might have to make. She tossed a cheerful good morning to the doctor and Jim and disappeared into the laboratory.

"Let's try those seals on bottles," the doctor said to Jim. "If they won't take a bottle—and I don't think they will—we'll have to get some milk down them some other way. They've hardly eaten anything for the last three days. You warm up two quarts of whole milk, and I'll measure out the corn oil."

For several years the doctor had been gathering information about the composition of various kinds of milk, and now he could rummage around in his file cabinet and come up with the formula for making artificial whale milk, monkey milk, seal milk, or almost any other kind of milk. He had learned that seal milk is extremely rich in fat. Ordinary cow's milk has only about four per cent, but seal milk has forty per cent. So the doctor knew that, in order to nourish the young seals properly, he would have to greatly increase the richness of the cow's milk. He carefully measured out the right amount of corn oil and poured it into the two quarts of milk that Jim was warming on the gas stove in the hospital kitchen.

The seal pups were hungry; there was no doubt about that.

They made grunting, whining noises and lifted their round heads eagerly when the doctor and Jim approached with the bottles they had prepared. But their eagerness disappeared when the heavy rubber nipples were offered to them. They shook their heads from side to side and backed away, even when the doctor squeezed out some of the warm, rich milk and let it fall on their lips. They simply hadn't learned how to suck on a nursing bottle.

"All right," the doctor said. "I didn't think it would work the first time. We'll have to get the milk down them through a tube. And then, Jim, you'll have to try them several times a day with ground-up fish mixed in the milk, until they learn to eat by themselves."

Jim had expected that he would get the job of teaching the seals to eat, so he was not surprised.

"Move them out of doors where we've got more room,"

the doctor said. "We're bound to spill some of the milk and you can hose down easier out there."

Moving the two babies out of doors was simple, for they were in a double cage, one part inside the hospital building and the other part outside. Jim rolled back the iron door between the two parts of the cage and dragged the seals' "bathtub" to the front of the outdoor half. The so-called bathtub was only a large, shallow tin tray that held a few inches of water. It wasn't deep enough for the seals to swim in; but they liked the feel of water around them, and they had stayed in it all the time they had been in the hospital.

While the doctor was in the hospital's pharmacy, fitting a narrow glass funnel into a piece of rubber tube, Jim found an old animal crate and turned it upside down on the walk outside the hospital, to make a sort of table. The seals, he knew, were quite friendly and not inclined to bite, so he simply picked one up in his arms, carried it out of the cage, and placed it on the box. It lay there quietly, looking around with interest, and even began to grow drowsy as Jim stroked its wet, smooth neck.

The doctor came out a moment later with his tube, two big cups of the warm milk, and a towel. Jim wrapped the towel around the seal's neck so that his hands would not slip when he held its head upright. Then, as the startled seal opened its mouth to complain about this unusual treatment, the doctor slipped the small rubber tube into its mouth and gently worked it down into its throat a few inches, taking care not to block its breathing.

Next, working quickly, he poured warm milk into the funnel and loosened a clamp on the tube. The milk flowed

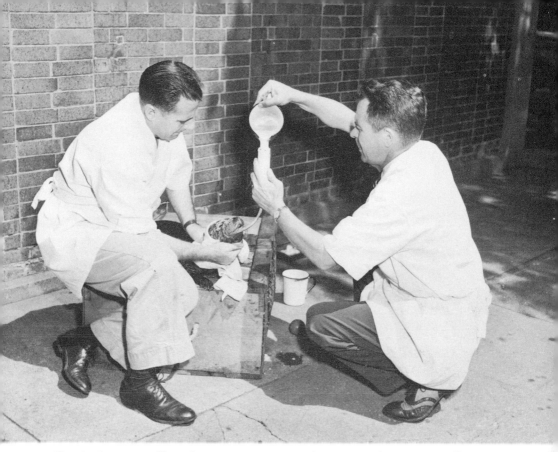

slowly but steadily down into the seal's stomach. It was all over in two minutes—and one of the youngsters had had its first good meal in several days.

The feeding of the second seal was even quicker. Both little seals belched a few times—their way of saying thank you, said the doctor, who now left Jim to put them back in their bathtub. It was time for the doctor to begin his morning rounds of the animal buildings.

From the floor beside his desk he picked up his little black bag. It contained rolls of sterile bandages, surgical scissors, adhesive tape, penicillin ointment, and other odds and ends of small supplies. The doctor had carried that bag so long that he hardly felt dressed without it. Bag swinging, he hurried out to the animal ambulance that stood in front of the hospital.

This morning he intended to visit only one or two of the buildings where he had treated patients the day before. It would have been almost as fast to walk to them, but he preferred to drive the ambulance, a small automobile with a green cross and the words *New York Zoological Society Animal Ambulance* painted on its sides. Bottles of sterile saline and disinfecting solutions, nets and ropes for restraining animals, heavy leather gloves, and rubber boots—all representing emergency equipment—were neatly stowed in racks in the car. With the little black bag *and* the ambulance, the doctor could get to any part of the zoo in a very short time and arrive prepared for at least minor emergencies.

His first stop was at the bear dens. Joe, the keeper of the bears, was washing down the floor of one of the rock dens with a fire hose. He shut off the water as the ambulance approached.

"There he is, Doc. His nose started running yesterday afternoon and it's worse this morning. Maybe he's got a little cold."

"I expect so," said the doctor. "Anyway, I think we can cure him quickly enough. How's he on sweet things?"

"Like all bears. Can't get enough."

"All right. You come over to the hospital in half an hour and I'll have something ready for you."

The next stop was the Great Apes House. Nobody was sick there; the only trouble was that Andy, the orangutan, was too healthy. Or, at least, he had too big an appetite. Andy had come to the zoo as a tiny, appealing baby, and he had

been petted and pampered and fed all sorts of delicacies. He was still the pet of all the keepers in the Great Apes House, and the doctor suspected that they were giving him even more than the ten pounds of fruit and vegetables he was supposed to get each morning and afternoon. At any rate, Andy had been putting on so much weight in the last few months that now he was almost too fat to walk. The doctor had given strict instructions the day before that Andy's daily ration of food was to be reduced by three pounds, and he wondered how Andy had accepted the radical change in his diet.

"Any trouble with Andy, Mickey?" he asked the keeper.

"Doctor, it's breaking my heart, that it is! That Andy boy, he can't live on just seventeen pounds a day! He follows me around, just begging for something to eat. How long are we going to keep this up, Doc?"

The doctor laughed. Mickey, he knew, had been the one who had spoiled Andy, bringing him out-of-season grapes and peaches and increasing his daily food allowance until the young ape was almost a caricature of what an orangutan ought to be.

"Mickey, this is the best thing that's happened to Andy since you took charge of him. He won't starve. Don't you worry about that! Just keep it up a few more weeks and then we'll see. He seems bright enough this morning, I must say."

"Oh, he's bright, my boy Andy is. But he's hungry, Doc. You wouldn't think I could give him maybe a little handful of bananas in the middle of the morning . . .?"

"No, I certainly wouldn't." The doctor hurried away, for he knew that if he didn't Mickey would keep on trying to coax a few more pounds of food for his darling Andy. And Andy just had to get some of that fat off.

He turned the ambulance around and drove to the Zebra House for a quick look at the colt that had been born two days before. This morning it was trotting alongside its mother on its spindly legs, seemingly so fragile and yet so steady and sure. The colt was all right. No trouble there.

Before the day was over the doctor would try to find time to visit all the other animal buildings, to talk to the keepers and cast his own appraising eye over the health of their animals. But now he had to take care of that black bear with the running nose. . . . And something ought to be done soon about those musk oxen and their hoofs. . . . And there was all the morning mail . . . and probably a dozen people had telephoned and wanted him to call back. He turned back to the hospital.

The bear keeper was waiting for him, so the doctor went to the drug room for a bottle of white powder and sent Jim to the cook room for a pound of strained honey.

"How much do you figure that bear weighs, Joe?"

"Oh . . . hundred and fifty, maybe a hundred and seventy-five."

"Nearer a hundred and seventy-five, I'd say. That'll mean

. . . let's see . . . just about ten grams of sulfanilamide for a good dose."

Into the can of honey the doctor dumped nearly a cupful of the dried sulfa and stirred it thoroughly until the white crystals were thoroughly mixed in.

"There you are, Joe. Get a long-handled spoon from the cook room and give him a quarter of it now and the rest at noon, midafternoon, and just before you go home. Let him eat it all and lick the can, if he wants to. I'll have a look to-morrow morning and see how he's doing, but I expect we'll have to do this for the next three days."

"Thanks, Doc."

Modern miracle drugs certainly made a veterinarian's job a lot easier, the zoo doctor reflected. A handful of sulfa powder in honey, and the bear would be cured—unless, as was very unlikely, there were complications. It was a lot easier than having to give him a hypodermic injection or forcing bad-tasting medicine down his throat. The bear would take his medicine willingly and even eagerly, and a cure would follow almost automatically.

The rest of the morning went just about the way the doctor thought it would. There were letters to answer. There were telephone calls to make to the curators of the mammal and bird and reptile departments of the zoo, all of them about some small matter of diet or illness that must be attended to. But, to the doctor's surprise, he got through his morning's work in time to join the other members of the zoo staff at luncheon in one of the zoo's restaurants—something he was seldom able to do, for emergencies always seemed to arise at just about lunch time.

It was the curator of mammals who decided the doctor's afternoon work for him. "The carpenter shop phoned me this morning about that special crate for the musk oxen," he said. "It's finally finished."

"Good!" said the doctor. "You have it delivered to the musk-ox corral by one o'clock, and by two o'clock I'll have the job done . . . I hope." That *would* be a relief. Weeks ago he had noticed that the musk oxen were developing overgrown hoofs, and he had been waiting for the overworked carpenter shop to build a special kind of crate that he and the curator of mammals had designed. This crate was merely a long, narrow, slatted box, hinged at the bottom of one side. When a musk ox had been induced to enter it, heavy straps would be passed around its body until it was securely fastened to the hinged side. Then the locks at the top of that side would be loosened, it would be lowered to the ground, and the musk ox would be in a position to have its feet examined and treated, without any of the rough handling that used to be necessary.

It was high time he went to work on those feet, too, for the hard hoofs had "snowshoed"; that is, they had turned forward and upward from continued growth. On the hard, frozen, rocky earth in Greenland, the musk oxen would have kept their hoofs in perfect condition by pawing at the ice and snow to uncover and eat the lichens on the ground. But here in the zoo, where they no longer had to eat lichens under the ice, they had lost the habit of pawing at the ground and wearing their hoofs down. So every six months or so their hoofs had to be trimmed back to their original shape.

The doctor remembered several times when he and a crew

of keepers had struggled for half a day just to drive a musk ox into a corner and get enough ropes around it to hold it still for a few minutes. Then other men had to rush in and push the snorting, struggling animal over until it was lying on its side. It was hot, heavy, dangerous work and once or twice the doctor himself had narrowly missed being gored by one of the swinging horns. It was just pure luck that nobody had ever been hurt in the performance of this necessary job. Now, with the new crate, it ought to be as simple as trimming a pony's hoofs.

Fortunately, the zoo's musk-ox herd was not a large one—just two adults and two calves. The doctor noticed that the two calves suspected something unusual was about to happen. When he arrived at the corral, the youngsters were standing side by side in the doorway of their shelter house, staring unblinkingly at the men moving the heavy crate into the yard. Those babies would stand their ground, too, in the face of any danger—heads out, facing the enemy. That was the way with musk oxen, even when the "enemy" was a friend coming to help them. The doctor was glad to see that the youngsters' hoofs were all right. They wouldn't need to be trimmed for another six months, perhaps.

The two adult musk oxen were in one of the compartments in their house. So under the doctor's direction the crate, its end gate lifted, was set up to block the doorway. Then, with a broom, a keeper made a threatening gesture, and one of the musk oxen bolted through the doorway and into the crate. He must have seen the crate in his path, but in true musk-ox fashion he decided to crash through it. The crate, however, happened to be even stronger than a musk ox. In a fraction

of a second the gate was dropped behind him, and he was trapped. Broad bands of webbing were passed around his body, and when he was securely lashed to the movable side of the crate, it was lowered to the floor.

Now the work could begin. First the matted, unshed hair on the musk ox's body and legs was cut away. "We'll give him a beauty treatment while we're about it," the doctor said. Then he went to work on the feet. With the musk ox tied down this way, it was really no more difficult than trimming the hoofs of a horse, and in a few minutes the doctor had all four hoofs cut down to their normal shape and size. When the job was done, it was a simple matter to raise the hinged side of the crate, roll the crate back to the door of the side room, untie the bands of webbing, and lift the end gate. Instantly the musk ox, unharmed but furious, plunged forward —at liberty again.

When he had taken care of the first musk ox, the doctor took time out to telephone the curator of mammals and report the success of their new idea. "Everything worked just the way we thought it would," he said. "It was no trouble at all. The animal walked right in, we tied him and let him down, and I got those hoofs back in shape in twenty minutes. That's a wonderful crate. We ought to get a patent on it."

That was at two o'clock.

At seven o'clock that night the doctor gave up and went home. The second musk ox had seen how her mate was trapped, and nothing would induce her to go into the crate.

It was almost a month later when at last she forgot her fears, and the doctor could finally finish the job he had started with such confidence.

# Doctoring an Elephant

Sudana was sick.

The zoo doctor heard about it from the gateman when he drove into the zoo that morning. He heard about it again from the keeper of the Penguin House, who shouted that he was wanted over at the Elephant House right away. And he got the news a third time from Jim as he drew up in front of the low-roofed, secluded Animal Hospital in the center of the zoo.

The hospital attendant was dragging out a hose to wash down the animal cages at the front of the hospital, but he dropped his work and hurried over. "Bob says will you please come over to the Elephant House right away. Sudana's not acting right, and he doesn't know what to do."

"Maybe I won't either."

"You?" Jim didn't believe that. "You'll give her a pill, and she'll be out begging peanuts in a week."

"What are you trying to do, Jim—promote a raise?"

"I'll take the raise if you've got one to give away, but I bet you'll fix her up pretty quick, anyhow."

"We'll see. Elephants don't get sick easily, and they don't cure easily."

While he was talking, the doctor entered the Animal Hospital and hung up his coat. Then he slipped into a short, freshly laundered white gown. Jim had to tie it in the back for him. Despite all his years of doing the most delicate surgery on mammals and birds and reptiles, the doctor was all thumbs when it came to knotting a bow tie or tying the strings of his hospital gown behind his back.

Since three people had been told to let him know about Sudana's illness as soon as he arrived, the doctor gathered that the matter was rather pressing. He snatched up his black bag of emergency medicines, hurried out to the animal ambulance, and roared away. As it turned out, he didn't need either the black bag or the ambulance in treating Sudana. He needed a lot of other things, though—especially ingenuity.

Bob, the Elephant House keeper, came out to meet him as he drew up at the front door. "I'm glad you're here, Doc. Sudana's mighty sick."

"When did all this happen?"

"In the night, I guess. Last evening I left her half a bale of timothy hay and six loaves of bread and one bucket of potatoes, like always, and I filled her water trough. She didn't eat hardly anything in the night, and this morning she kept acting as if she wanted water. I filled the trough twice and she kept begging for more, but I didn't think she ought to drink so much all at once. And she feels all hot."

"Hmm. Let's have a look."

Sudana certainly did look sick. Something was wrong inside those four tons of flesh and bone. The big African elephant was leaning, actually leaning—a thing she never did when she was her usual sturdy self—against the steel bars at the front of her compartment in the Elephant House. Her enormous ears were folded back against her neck and shoulders, and not once did she flap them in greeting to her friend the doctor. Most ominous of all, her normally restless tail hung straight down, never once twitching the curved brush of hairs at the tip.

"What's the matter, old girl? This isn't like you, Sudana.

You've never given me a bit of trouble in twenty years!" The doctor talked steadily and soothingly while he slowly, deliberately, without any sudden motions, climbed over the guardrail and reached through the bars to lay a hand on the elephant's trunk. He felt it in several places and then slipped his hand under her ear and down the length of her rough foreleg and back along her body. It was like rubbing coarsely finished cement—warm cement. Sudana had a fever, and a high one.

The doctor stepped back over the guardrail. "You gave her a couple of big drinks this morning?"

"She wanted more. She trumpeted until she pretty nearly busted my eardrums, and then she backed up against that iron plate in the wall and banged on it until you could hear her all over the zoo."

"All right, don't give her any more water. We've got to get some medicine into her, and she isn't going to like the taste of it; but if she's thirsty enough maybe she'll take it in her drinking water."

"I hate not giving her a drink, but I guess it's for her own good. O.K., Doc."

The doctor perched on the guardrail opposite Sudana's compartment and watched her carefully for a few minutes, considering how to handle this very unwieldy patient. It was important to figure out her weight pretty carefully, for the amount of sulfadiazine he intended to give her would be calculated on the basis of so many grams per hundred pounds of elephant. For a good many years now, there hadn't been any means of weighing Sudana. When she first came to the zoo from the Sudan in 1931 she was just a teen-ager, not too big to be shipped in a crate; and it had been a simple matter to put her on the scales. She had weighed 1,975 pounds, as the doctor recalled it.

But what about now, twenty-five years later? Well, the doctor remembered old Alice, for forty years the queen (and an imperious queen, too) of the zoo's elephant herd. When Alice died, her body was taken away on a truck, and it was possible to weigh her; she weighed 7,033 pounds. Alice had been taller, but maybe not quite as bulky as Sudana. No, definitely not as bulky, for she had seemed to shrink in her last, arthritis-ridden years. The doctor made a guess. Eight thousand pounds, more or less, was what Sudana must weigh now. It was only a guess, but there wasn't a chance of getting a more accurate figure.

Eight thousand pounds . . . eighty units of a hundred pounds each . . . six grams of sulfadiazine per hundredweight. Whew! That meant four hundred and eighty grams of the drug that he'd have to get into Sudana somehow. About four cupfuls!

With a wave of the hand to Bob, who was talking to Sudana and explaining why she couldn't have a drink of water right away, the doctor walked thoughtfully out of the Elephant House and drove back to the hospital in the ambulance. It was too bad that Bob had already given Sudana so much water. Even with her high fever, she wouldn't take unlimited quantities, and maybe she wouldn't drink at all if the water tasted too strongly of the medicine. She was a smart elephant.

Well, the only thing was to try her and see. If she wouldn't take the drug in her drinking water, he'd have to figure out some other way.

Jim was busy with his morning chore—cleaning the cages

of the hospital's patients—when the doctor returned. A Hima-
layan tahr was the only large patient; its flanks had been
slashed by the horns of a rival. A Pondicherry vulture was
hopping about its cage despite the splint and bandage around
one leg with a damaged tendon.

In the laboratory the nurse was immersed in the task the
doctor had given her—pouring hot agar into sterile Petri
dishes and keeping them covered until the gelatinous amber
stuff cooled and stiffened.

"As soon as you finish, weigh out four hundred and
eighty grams of sulfadiazine and make three equal packages
of it," the doctor said.

"Four hundred and eighty grams? Why, that's enough for
an elephant!"

"It *is* for an elephant—Sudana. Don't hurry; I won't want
it until about noon."

The nurse was a good technician. She would weigh out
the dosage to the last grain. The doctor left her to her work
and settled behind his desk to attack the morning mail and
the telephone messages awaiting him.

He had forgotten all about the clock and was just starting
to dictate a long autopsy report on a lesser panda when the
nurse appeared at his office door. "Those three packages of
sulfadiazine are on the pharmacy table," she said. "I'm going
to lunch now, unless you want me for something."

"Lunch?" The doctor looked at his watch. "Say! Sudana
will certainly be thirsty by this time. Glad you reminded me."

It was almost one o'clock. The doctor apologized to his
secretary for keeping her so long beyond her lunch hour.
His own lunch did not matter; he was used to eating at odd

times, or not eating at all if he had a long job on his hands. He would have to skip lunch today, for it was important to start Sudana's medication right away.

A few minutes later he was at the Elephant House. Bob was sitting on the guardrail staring glumly at Sudana. And Sudana was certainly not getting any better. She looked even sicker and more woebegone than she had four hours before.

"This has been a rough morning, Doc. She keeps feeling the water trough with her trunk, and then she looks at me, and I can hardly stand it."

"You didn't give her any, did you? Honest, now?"

"Not a drop. I feel like a heel, but I didn't give her any, just like you said."

"I know it's hard on you and on Sudana, too; but she's a mighty sick elephant, and this is the surest way I know to get that medicine down her. Now you run her into the next stall, so she can't see me while I mix the medicine in her water."

Bob turned the wheel that slowly opened the door between Sudana's compartment and the stall next door. Sudana watched him with indifference. She saw no reason to move from one stall where she was unhappy to another one where she would be no happier. It was not until Bob picked up the hose and pretended to be filling the water trough next door that Sudana lumbered through the doorway. Quickly he closed the connection between the two stalls.

"Good! Now bring your hose and we'll give her a drink— and hope she'll take it."

The doctor opened one of the packages the nurse had prepared, and spilled the white powder into Sudana's drinking trough. By means of vigorous stirring he mixed it thoroughly with the water. "We'll have to give her the dose in three parts. I'm a little afraid she'll taste it even in a one-third dilution like this, and she certainly would if we dumped the whole dose in at once. Well, it's the best we can do. Open up, and let her come back."

Sudana smelled the water. She squeezed through the door even before it was fully opened and headed straight for her water trough, trunk outstretched. Dipping its tip deeply, she drew up a couple of gallons, and curled her trunk to eject the cool fluid into her parched mouth.

What was this?

Water dribbled from her mouth. Her trunk continued to squirt the liquid onto her tongue, but something was wrong. *Very* wrong! Somebody was playing a mean trick!

Violently Sudana's trunk jerked out of her mouth, and medicated water gushed from her lower lip. She aimed her trunk at the doctor and her perfidious keeper. They ducked, but it was too late. They got the full effects of a gallon of cold sulfadiazine-and-water straight in their faces.

Serves me right for tricking her! was Bob's unspoken comment as he and the doctor fled from a second blast.

So *that* didn't work! was what the doctor said to himself. Now what do we do?

While they sponged the medicated water from their faces and clothes over the sink in the keepers' room, the doctor and Bob held a council of war.

"She likes ice cream, doesn't she?"

"She's crazy about it. People give her ice-cream cones and she never gets enough."

"Well, we might try filling her up for once. Now here's

how we'll work it. I'll mix her medicine in a quart of ice cream. She's suspicious of you and me; we tricked her with that water, and she'll remember it. But I'll have Jim come over and feed her the stuff in ice-cream cones!"

Bob beamed. "That'll do the trick, Doc! You send Jim over. I'll stay out of sight."

Back at the hospital, the doctor ordered a quart of chocolate ice cream and a box of cones. "Change into your street clothes," he told Jim. "I want you to stand around in the crowd, like any visitor, and offer these cones to Sudana. As far as she'll know, you'll be just a visitor with something good to eat."

While Jim was changing his clothes, so he would look like a zoo visitor, the doctor prepared Sudana's cones. First he set aside enough plain ice cream to fill two of them. Then he mixed a full dose of sulfadiazine into the rest of the ice cream,

which filled quite a pile of cones. He put them back in the box and placed the cones without any medicine on top.

"She's a smart elephant and you'll have to outsmart her," the doctor told Jim. "Walk over to the Elephant House and stand well back until you see a dozen or so visitors feeding the elephants. Then walk up closer. Hold out one of these two cones on the top, until Sudana reaches for it. Let her have both of them; they don't have any medicine, so she'll swallow them and reach for more. Then give her the medicated ones as fast as you can get her to take them."

"I'm just a visitor with more ice-cream cones than I know what to do with, huh?"

"That's the idea. Bob will stay out of sight, and I'll wait here at the hospital. We don't want to let *anything* make her suspicious."

"Sounds easy enough."

As Jim left the hospital with the box of cones under his arm, the doctor telephoned the Elephant House. "Jim's on his way. This time I think we'll fool her. I'll stay here until he comes back."

He didn't have long to wait. In five minutes Jim was back. The front of his shirt and most of his coat were dripping with melted chocolate ice cream and sulfadiazine!

There was, the doctor finally admitted to himself, only one thing left to do: go and give Sudana a whopping big injection —he made a rapid calculation—of about sixteen million units of penicillin. A hypodermic injection was the only *sure* way of getting medicine into her, and it would have to be penicillin instead of sulfadiazine. It would be easier to inject, and just as effective. Yes, it was the only sure way—*if* she'd stand for being jabbed with a long and sharp needle . . . *if* he could get through the skin on the first try . . . *if* she didn't move her leg—even if only a few inches—at the critical second of injection and snap the needle off . . . *if*—

Well, there was no use figuring "if's." It had to be done, one way or another; or else, in a couple of days, the mammal department would have to scratch one elephant off its list. The doctor knew only too well what was the matter with Sudana. She had picked up a virulent streptococcus infection. He had seen the same thing happen to an elephant nearly twenty years ago. Those were the days before miracle drugs, and there was nothing anybody could do. The whole zoo staff stood around helplessly while gentle little Congo simply lay down and died.

If you could only *talk* to an elephant and make it understand that the evil-tasting medicine was for its own good! The doctor remembered a magazine article he had once read, written by a woman. She claimed that her dog always trusted her to do the right thing when it got sick; that animals "understood" that a veterinarian might have to hurt them to make them well. Maybe dogs understood, the doctor thought (although he doubted it), but elephants certainly didn't. It would be mighty convenient if they did!

Now that he was down to his last resort, the doctor worked swiftly. He gathered together half a dozen vials of penicillin, a giant hypodermic syringe, a handful of gauze pads, and a bottle of sterilizing alcohol, and put them in his bag. In a few minutes he was back at the Elephant House. "How about it? Can you get her to hold still for about fifteen seconds?"

Bob was doubtful. "That's a long time for an elephant to hold still. I could try her with a bucket of apples. That's a treat she doesn't get very often. Is it going to hurt her?"

"Not really. Not as much as it would hurt you or me."

"Well . . ."

"We've got to try, anyhow. You keep her busy for fifteen seconds, maybe less—just long enough for me to push the plunger on this syringe."

"If you say so, Doc. But be ready to jump if she doesn't like it."

"I don't figure on having to jump. You keep shoving those apples into her."

While the keeper went to the feed room and filled a bucket with apples, the doctor plunged the needle of the syringe into vial after vial of penicillin and withdrew the calculated dose—sixteen million units. Like the sulfadiazine, the penicillin was figured on an estimated weight of eight thousand pounds. Then he saturated a pile of gauze pads with alcohol, for scrubbing and sterilizing the site of the injection — the "armpit" of Sudana's left foreleg, where the skin was comparatively thin. She was visibly more listless. The fever was wearing her down, and in another few hours she would be too sick and apathetic to care whether the needle pricked her or not. She might feel it now, but the doctor was confident Bob could control her. He was a good keeper; he liked his animals and was sensitive to their moods.

"I'm ready, Bob. Start feeding her."

Bob squirmed between the bars and set the bucket down in front of Sudana. "Steady, girl! Apples, Sudana! Steady now!"

The great gray bulk shuffled forward a few feet, and Sudana's trunk explored the rim of the bucket. Bob held an apple so her trunk could curl around it, and swiftly she tucked it into her mouth. A faint crunch showed that she was enjoying it.

"All right, Doc."

Sudana was reaching for another apple when the doctor stepped between the bars and entered her stall. One eye rolled in his direction, but she made no move.

"Don't talk to her, Doc. Just do your stuff and get out as fast as you can. I've got her steady."

The gauze pads reeked of raw alcohol. The liquid dripped cold from his fingers. It would feel good on Sudana's harsh, hot skin—if her hide was sensitive enough to feel anything as mild as a few degrees of coolness.

The doctor felt quickly under the foreleg, probing with skilled fingers. Here was a hard spot, here a softer one, here the softest of all. Pressing hard on the gauze, he swabbed and scrubbed the site until the alcohol had penetrated every crack and fold.

All right—let her have it. He pinched the gray skin into a broad fold and with one swift motion plunged the needle as deep as it would go. With the same motion his thumb began pushing the plunger downward.

Sudana flinched. The thick skin rippled under the doctor's fingers; for a split second the hypodermic syringe trembled in his hand, and he thought the needle might break. But he rocked the syringe with the movement of the skin, and the plunger sank steadily downward.

"Steady, Sudana! Steady, girl. Here's another apple. Steady,

now." Bob's calm, soothing voice droned on, and just as rhythmically Sudana's trunk dipped into the bucket, rose to her mouth, and dipped into the bucket again.

"We're still all right, Doc, but you better hurry. I can see the bottom of the bucket."

Another quarter inch to go. The doctor pressed the plunger evenly and smoothly—and it was done! A quick tug, and the shining needle came out. Only a drop of the white fluid marked the site of the injection. In another two seconds the doctor dabbed the site with the gauze, squeezing the tiny lips of the puncture together. A few seconds more, and he had walked around Sudana's head and was out in the hall.

Bob stood up at the same instant, spilling the last two apples on the floor. "Just in time, Doc," he said. "Did you give her the full dose?"

"Sixteen million units, right down to the last one."

"That'll cure her, huh?"

"I think she'll be all right. Her fever ought to come down tonight. Give her a light feeding and all the water she wants. I'll look in tomorrow and repeat the dose if I have to, but she ought to be O.K. in a few days."

The doctor wrapped the needle of his syringe in the gauze pads and laid it in the little black bag. "She's a grand old girl, but she's too smart for her own good."

The low, mournful toot of the five o'clock whistle floated across the zoo.

"And I was going to run tests on four chimpanzees this afternoon! Well, they can wait, and Sudana couldn't. And I guess she's worth a day's work!"

# Four Little Women from Africa

The doctor worried about Sudana for a day or two, but then her appetite came back and she began tucking away a hundred and twenty-five pounds of hay, grain, bread, and vegetables every day, plus all the peanuts and popcorn and crackerjack she could beg from visitors. He still stopped at the Elephant House for a few minutes on his daily rounds, but he was no longer concerned. Sudana was going to be all right. What worried the doctor was himself. What was the matter with *him*? For the first time in his life he was having chimpanzee trouble.

What made it so baffling was that there seemed to be nothing unusual about those four baby chimpanzees newly arrived from Africa. He just glanced at them on the afternoon they came in, to make sure they had food and water and bedding. The four huddled little black creatures stared at him with soft brown eyes, never moving. Just some more baby chimpanzees, to be X-rayed for possible chest infections, examined for blood and intestinal parasites, shifted to a new diet perhaps. . . . It was all utterly routine.

Of course, in one way these really were rather special baby chimpanzees. They had been given the names of Amy, Beth, Jo, and Meg, after the characters in Louisa M. Alcott's book, *Little Women;* and those names caught the fancy of some newspaper reporters, so the babies had received a good deal of publicity even before they arrived. Naturally, the mammal department wanted the tests rushed so the Little Women could go on exhibition as soon as possible.

But the way things are going, thought the doctor, I'll be lucky to get these tests run off by next fall. I must be doing something wrong, and I'm blessed if I know what it is.

He had just spent an entire morning trying to make a superficial examination of the babies' skin and teeth.

The trouble didn't start until the doctor began his examination. As always, when he had one of these thorough inspections to make, he laid out his instruments in the surgery and told Jim and the nurse to bring the animal in. They didn't have the slightest difficulty. They simply went into the quarantine cage, took one of the babies by the hand, and led it down the hall to the surgery—no trouble at all.

But the moment the doctor leaned forward with the thermometer or tongue depressor or hypodermic syringe, those tame, friendly, gentle, trusting, affectionate Little Women reverted to their jungle ways. They screeched, they bit, they fought with all their strength and every defensive weapon at their command. Once or twice it took the combined strength

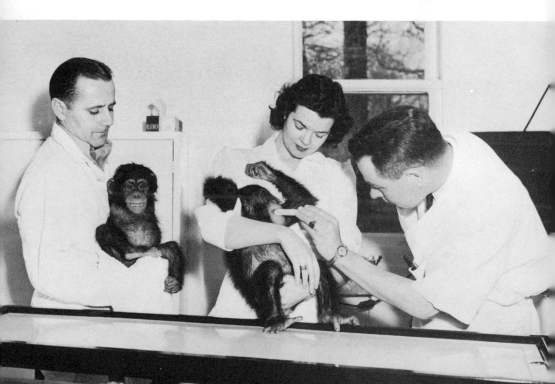

of Jim and the nurse to keep a baby from breaking loose. In twenty years of practice in the zoo, the doctor had never before seen baby chimpanzees throw such tantrums.

It was no use going on with the examination under those conditions.

"Take her away and let her calm down," the doctor told Jim after the second failure. "She's afraid of me, but maybe she'll get over it."

It bothered him to have an animal afraid of him. Inevitably some of them were, of course, for almost every wild animal has in its make-up an impulse to flee—or to attack—if a human being crosses the invisible but nevertheless definite line that separates "safety" from "danger." Animal psychologists call it the flight distance. Usually those invisible lines are all out of their natural proportions in a zoo. The animals become so accustomed to their keepers and visitors—and the protection of bars or moats—that they permit closer approach than they would in the wild. But some seem to have no flight distance at all, at least when they are babies. Little chimpanzees, for instance, normally *want* human companionship. The doctor had had chimpanzee trouble before, but it was always the opposite kind: the babies wanted to cling to him, and sometimes he had to push them away to make room for his examination.

The reason for his trouble with the Little Women was a riddle he couldn't solve, but he determined to overcome the situation some way. He could, of course, make his examinations in spite of the babies' protests. He could call in another keeper to help Jim, if necessary. But he didn't like to go to such an extreme. Chimpanzees and gorillas and orangutans, in particular, are very much like human beings in some respects. They remember things like that. If he forced the Little Women to submit, they might never forget it, and as long as they lived in the zoo they would be afraid of him and resist treatment of any kind.

It did vaguely cross the doctor's mind that the whole thing was unnatural, that the four little chimpanzees were acting as if they had had previous experience with a veterinarian and that it hadn't been pleasant. But of course there was no way of finding out anything about their past history, before they came to the zoo. The only thing on the zoo's records, as the doctor knew, was a letter from an animal dealer in Africa saying he had four baby chimpanzees he could supply. The zoo had ordered them by cable, and they had duly arrived. That was all anybody knew about them.

When in doubt, use your head, the doctor advised himself. The other day I found a way of getting medicine into a middle-aged elephant. I'd hate to think four baby chimpanzees can keep me from doing my job.

Force was no good; it might only make them fear him forever. But kindness might be the answer. If he could manage to gain their trust and natural affection, the present examination and any further treatment through the years would be easy.

He decided to postpone the tests for a few days. The curator of mammals would have a tantrum, but he could cope with the curator's tantrum more easily than he could with a baby chimpanzee's. In the next few days, he resolved, he would make friends with these four Little Women.

It wasn't easy. It wasn't dignified. It wasn't conducive to

normal hospital routine. But for the next few days the doctor devoted himself wholeheartedly to gaining the affection and trust of those four young animals. It had been Jim's job to take complete care of them, but the doctor relieved Jim of all responsibility. He came to the zoo half an hour early each morning so he could clean the chimpanzee compartment before the regular feeding hour. He prepared their food himself, chopping the fruits and vegetables and carrying the pans of food and water into the compartment. He brought grapes and bits of overripe banana and lumps of sugar—every special delicacy that baby chimpanzees are known to like.

He made progress, too.

"You know, Doc," Jim said to him at the end of the second day, "you're doin' pretty good. In another six months you'll be as good at this job as I am! Why, today one of those babies actually didn't try to bite you when you offered her a grape!"

It didn't take the six months that Jim had predicted. It took less than a week. Every morning between eight-thirty and nine-thirty the doctor swept the floor of the chimpanzee compartment and carried out the spilled and wasted food of the night before, brought fresh food and fresh water, changed the straw bedding in the little sleeping boxes, and talked baby talk to the babies. He stroked and petted them gently when they came within reach (always remembering to jerk his hand away if a tantrum of rage or fear seemed on the point of erupting), and gradually he came to be accepted as a friend. He couldn't, of course, spend all day playing with the babies. A certain amount of office work had to be performed, and

routine calls at the animal buildings had to be made. But it happened to be a comparatively quiet time, with no major accidents or illnesses, and the doctor's friendship with the chimpanzees prospered accordingly. The time finally came when they ran to him when he entered the quarantine ward, and the doctor (who had thought he was completely calm and professional as far as any animal was concerned) was thrilled when one of the babies actually leaped into his arms one morning and wrapped her arms around his neck.

It had taken almost a week, but it was worth it. The routine tests, which hadn't turned out to be so routine, finally were accomplished with ease and dispatch. Beth, it is true, squirmed and waved her arms and legs when the doctor tried

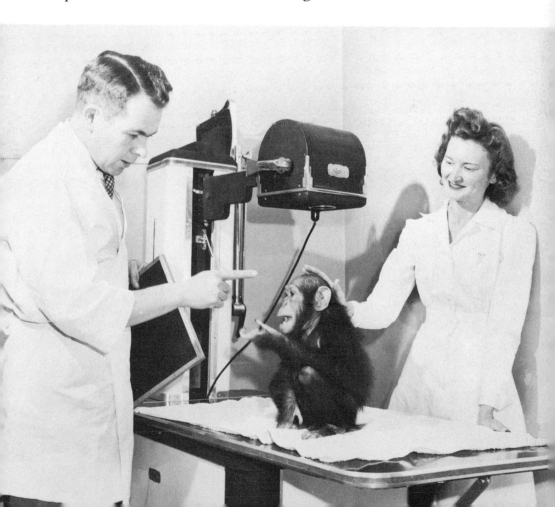

to insert a tongue depressor between her teeth, but everybody kept calm and the doctor talked baby talk to her ("Whazza mazzer wizzums, huh? Whazzer mazzer?") until the nurse threatened to have hysterics, for she had never heard the doctor talk baby talk to his patients before. But finally she calmed down, and Beth calmed down, and it all went off quite nicely. The other three Little Women made no objection to having their throats looked at. Jo was positively co-operative while the doctor was taking her temperature. Amy was just a trifle uncertain whether the X-ray machine was something she ought to be afraid of, when it came her turn to have her chest picture taken; but her friend the doctor convinced her that playtime was coming very soon, if she was a good girl, and that nothing was going to hurt her.

All the Little Women passed their hospital tests and (a week late) were turned over to the mammal department for exhibition. The doctor felt it was quite a triumph for his persistence and patience—in fact, a minor but very definite red-letter event in his career.

It was nearly six months later that a staff luncheon was held at the zoo for a party of foreign research men, and the doctor happened to be seated beside a thin, tanned young man who remarked that he had been doing malaria research on the west coast of Africa.

"And by the way, I met some old friends in your Great Apes House," he said. "Those young chimpanzees—the ones you call the Little Women. They were control animals in my laboratory for about six months, you know. I used them to supply samples of normal blood every ten days. Finally had to get rid of them, though. They got so they'd have tantrums every time they saw a doctor in a white gown. It was easy for us to get new chimpanzees, and since I knew the animal dealer would send them to some zoo, I figured it wouldn't matter. They didn't cause you any trouble, I hope."

The doctor was loyal to his Little Women. "Not the slightest," he said.

# Panda up a Tree

The doctor was making his early-morning rounds of the Bronx Zoo's animal buildings when he saw it. He jammed on the brakes of the animal ambulance so hard that he nearly pitched through the windshield.

Dolly, the larger of the two giant pandas—the rarest and most valuable animals in the zoo—was sitting astraddle a limb of the hickory tree in her outdoor enclosure. Just sitting there enjoying the spring sunshine. Just sitting there thirty feet above a granite ledge that would certainly break every bone in her body if she slipped and fell.

Strictly speaking, the fact that Dolly was up a tree was nothing for the doctor to worry about. It was the responsibility of the curator of mammals to see that giant pandas didn't climb trees, that they got down safely if they did climb trees anyway, and to make sure they didn't find a way of doing it again. The curator of mammals would do enough worrying for everybody, the doctor knew. The doctor's own worries would start if Dolly didn't get down in one piece— if she slipped, or one of those slender branches snapped off.

Although, the doctor said to himself, studying the probable place where Dolly would land if she fell out of the tree, there'd really be no problem for me, because she'd certainly be a dead panda if she bounced off that ledge.

Dolly was enjoying herself—no doubt about that. She may have recognized her old friend the doctor, for she squirmed into a position from which she could look down. As far as the doctor could see, she was not holding on; she was just balancing herself on the slender, swaying branch.

The doctor turned the ambulance around and got out of sight as quickly as possible. He had a feeling that at any moment Dolly was going to take it into her head to wave at him, or maybe even jump.

The curator of mammals arrived in the next ten minutes, and he was doing plenty of worrying. For the moment, most of it was worry about getting the panda down safely. But he was puzzled, too, as to how she could have gotten up the tree in the first place.

It was supposed to be impossible for the zoo's giant pandas to climb that tree. The giant panda is a good natural climber, and in its native China it often climbs trees. Everyone in the zoo knew that, but just the same nobody wanted *these* pandas to climb *this* tree. If a giant panda slipped and fell out of a tree in China, nobody knew about it and nobody worried. But these giant pandas had been captured and brought to New York at considerable expense and risk, and it would be a real tragedy if an accident happened to them. So the trunk of the hickory tree in their enclosure had been carefully sheathed with sheet metal, painted more or less to match the bark, up to a point that no panda could possibly reach.

Vince, the keeper of the pandas, had his own idea about how she had managed to get up in the tree. "It must have been a kind of accident," he said. "Lots of times they climb on top of each other. One will be standing alongside the wall, and the other will come up and climb on her back. That's how it must have happened. Molly was standing alongside the tree, and Dolly climbed up on her for fun and kind of accidentally reached up above the tin."

Probably it did happen just that way. But now the question was how to get Dolly down safely.

If she climbed down she'd be sure to slip when she came to the sheet metal and couldn't dig her claws into it. She'd certainly fall the last few feet—and that might be serious, with the rock ledge right beside the tree.

What was needed was a kind of wooden ladder to get her down past the metal, and so a ten-foot section of tree trunk was leaned against the hickory and wedged firmly in place. Once she reached it, Dolly could walk down to the ground easily.

All these preparations for her safe descent she found very interesting. Peering down from her high perch, she squirmed uneasily at first, as the tree trunk was propped in place, but soon she lost interest and stretched out in a comfortable crotch. As far as the watchers on the ground could tell, she simply went to sleep.

Zoo visitors had plenty of suggestions about getting her down. They agreed that the best thing to do was to call the fire department. Firemen were always climbing trees and rescuing cats. Or maybe the firemen could spread their net, and somebody could shake the giant panda out of the tree and into it. The curator of mammals thanked everyone politely for these suggestions, but made no effort to call the fire department. There is, he knew, a good deal of difference between rescuing a two-pound cat and a hundred-pound giant panda. Cat scratches you can treat with iodine, but a giant panda's scratches generally require the attention of a surgeon.

It was Vince, the keeper, who came up with an idea that might work. "Remember last year how we gave them a big panda doll to play with?" he asked. "Well, Dolly up there— she's the boss. She wouldn't hardly let Molly play with that doll at all. Maybe if we got another doll, and let Molly play with it where Dolly could see her, she'd come down to chase Molly away."

"Good idea, Vince! That might work."

There was, as it happened, a gigantic panda doll in the Animal Nursery—a doll someone had presented as a toy for some of the baby animals to play with. Vince borrowed it and then, with much shouting and waving to attract Dolly's attention, he carried it to the foot of the tree. Then he opened the shelter door and let Molly come out.

The doll was a great success—for Molly. For the first time

she had full possession of a plaything without being dominated by Dolly. She chewed happily on its arms and legs, dragged it up and down the ledge and through the water of the little pool, and finally discarded it only when the stuffing began to spill out.

Dolly watched with mild interest for the first few minutes. And then she went back to sleep.

Noon came. Dolly changed position a few times, but always went back to sleep. Midafternoon came. Dolly roused enough to claw a few shreds of bark from the tree trunk and to break off a few twigs and chew on them absent-mindedly.

By this time Vince was worrying about the late-afternoon feeding. Dolly had had nothing to eat since breakfast. Molly had been given her usual handful of bamboo stalks for lunch, but now it was time for the late-afternoon portion of cornmeal mush. What, he asked the doctor, had he better do? Should he feed Molly and lock her up indoors for the night, and leave a pan of mush under the tree for Dolly in case she came down during the night? He hated to think of Dolly up there all night with nothing to eat.

The doctor had an inspiration. "Vince, you were telling me once about how you feed them in separate pans, and each one knows her own pan. . . ."

"That's right, Doc. I couldn't get two pans alike, so Molly gets her mush in an old galvanized pan, and Dolly's is white enamel. And they know which one's which, all right! That Molly—if she so much as lays a lip on Dolly's pan, Dolly's after her like a flash."

"O.K. You mix up a good feeding of mush in Dolly's pan, and you put it under the tree. Then you turn Molly out and let her eat out of Dolly's pan—and we'll see what happens."

"Doc, I think you've got something!"

In a few minutes Vince was back, with the white enamel pan overflowing with the corn-meal mush that both pandas relished. For good measure, he brought an armload of bamboo and scattered it on the paving. Even if jealousy didn't bring Dolly down, she might be hungry for her favorite bamboo, he figured.

The bamboo was wasted. Molly and the pan were enough. Dolly looked down with interest when Vince carried out the white pan, but her interest flamed into action when Molly

ambled toward it and began licking the mush. With as much ease and sureness as if she had been climbing that particular hickory tree all her life and knew every branch and twig, Dolly backed down the tree. Her feet never missed a sure resting place. She hugged the trunk and slid when she had to, and her hind feet felt unerringly for the slanting trunk that would carry her down from the top of the sheet iron. In a little more than three minutes she dropped the last two feet to the ground, whirled, and ran for the offending Molly. One swipe of her paw sent Molly sprawling. Molly scrambled to her feet and raced for the ledge, with Dolly behind her. Dolly caught up at the edge of the rock, and another blow tumbled Molly down the steep incline. Then, and not until then, did

Dolly stalk with dignity to her pan and lick up the remaining mush. Molly, that upstart, that highjacker, had been put in her place.

Dolly had a good, full feeding that night; but it took place inside the shelter house, behind locked doors. And she was not let out again the next day until the carpenters had added four feet of metal sheathing to the trunk of the hickory tree— right up to the first limbs.

It doesn't look very good, thought the doctor, but it's better to have a sheet of tin on a healthy hickory tree than splints on a crippled panda.

# Otto the Potto

The heroine of this story is the nurse in the Bronx Zoo's Animal Hospital, for the doctor himself said Otto the potto would have died if the nurse hadn't noticed what was happening and figured out what she ought to do.

It just goes to show that you've got to be thinking about your job and using your head every minute, if you're going to be good at the business of working with wild animals. And because the nurse did think about her job and use her head, the Bronx Zoo was the first zoo ever to raise a baby potto in captivity—and after its own mother had failed to do so.

Besides having a queer name, the potto is a queer animal. It's a small, soft-furred, honey-colored creature that sleeps all day in a tight ball in the crotch of a tree. Then, after dark, it climbs slowly and silently through the branches in search of fruit and leaves and insects. There are many other small creatures that sleep all day and hunt through the jungle by night, but the potto is different from all the rest in one special way: part of its skeleton almost sticks out of its fur.

On the back of its neck—just about where its back collar button would be if it wore an old-fashioned shirt with collar buttons—there is a little spur of bone sticking up under its skin. It's only about an eighth of an inch long, and you'd never see it unless you parted the fur with your fingers and looked carefully.

But if you do part the fur with your fingers, make sure the potto is very tame—or else be prepared to jerk your fingers away in a hurry. Slow and sluggish as the potto is when it is looking for food, it can turn and bite fiercely in a fraction of a second. That is one of the reasons why it is feared by so many natives in the Congo and why, in one part of Africa, it has a special name that means "the animal that bites and never lets go."

Otto's father and mother had had five babies before he was born, and all of them had died. They were all born at night, and when the keeper of the Small Mammal House came on duty in the morning he would usually find the babies dead on the floor of the compartment. Otto's mother never made the slightest effort to nurse any one of her babies or take care of it.

Otto might have died in the same way, except that the keeper came to work a little early on the morning after he was born, and just happened to look in the potto compartment almost as soon as he entered the building. He saw the tiny creature lying on the cold floor, and the father and mother asleep on the wooden platform above it. He picked up the baby and, to his surprise, found that it was still alive. There was still a chance of saving it, so he tucked it in his shirt to keep it warm and hurried to the Animal Hospital.

The doctor examined the baby carefully. There was no sign of injury. Its eyes were tight shut, its big hands and feet were drawn close to its breast, and its tiny, stubby tail was curled over the body as if to add its mite of warmth. But it had been thoroughly chilled by lying on the floor of the compartment and there was not a moment to lose.

The doctor called the nurse. "Fix up a heating pad in a box and get this baby warm while I make up a formula."

The doctor had no idea what the right formula for a baby potto might be, for nobody had ever tried to rear one before. But he reasoned that since the potto is a lowly, primitive member of the group to which the monkeys belong, a formula that would be good for a baby monkey might be good for it. So he made up a small bottle of the formula that scientists at Yale University had worked out for feeding the baby monkeys in their laboratory.

He had just finished mixing the formula when the nurse came into the diet kitchen.

"If you want to see something cute, Doctor," she said, "come look at Otto."

"Otto? Who's Otto?"

"Oh, that's what I'm going to call the new baby—the new potto. Otto the potto."

The doctor laughed and followed the nurse into her laboratory. She had lined the bottom and sides of a cardboard carton with an electric heating pad and built up a soft bed of cotton batting on the pad. Otto the potto was cradled in the batting, with a soft towel over him for a blanket. As a lid for the carton, the nurse had borrowed a small pane of glass from the zoo's carpentry shop. She had taped a thermometer inside the carton, where it could be read without lifting the glass, and the doctor noted that it read 80 degrees—just about right for a cold baby animal.

The nurse slid back the glass and lifted a corner of the towel. Otto was sound asleep, but his lips made quick, sucking motions.

"He's warm, but he's hungry."

"I've got his formula right here. Did you weigh him?"

"Yes—just under an ounce and a half."

"Good! Now, here's the formula. Try giving it to him with a medicine dropper, of course. He won't take much. You'll have to judge when to stop."

There wouldn't be much doubt about when to stop; Otto was so tiny that the nurse wondered whether one whole medicine dropper of milk might not be too much—almost enough

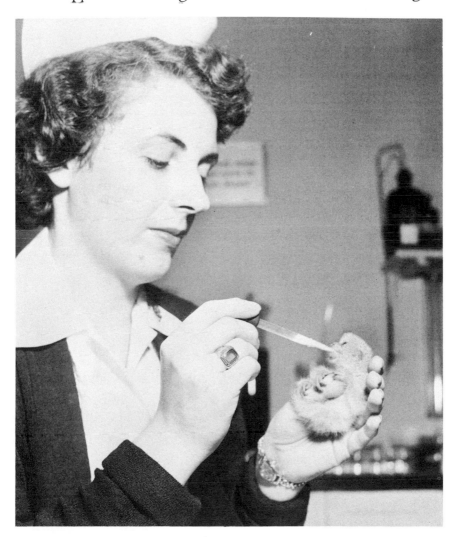

to drown him! She warmed the milk on a gas ring, filled a dropper, and tested one drop on her wrist. It was just warm enough.

Otto loved it. His mouth formed around the tip of the dropper and his tiny hands and feet curled tightly around the nurse's thumb. Gradually, drop by drop, the nurse squeezed out the milk and Otto took it all. He reached for the dropper and sucked harder when he came to the end, but that was all he was going to get for a first feeding. Resolutely the nurse nestled him in the cotton, covered him up, and slid the glass over the carton.

"How often, Doctor?"

"Every three hours. Right around the clock, I'm afraid. Can you manage it?"

"The girl who lives with me is going to love this—the alarm clock going off every three hours all night, and me getting up to feed a baby potto! But I'd sure like to try pulling this one through."

Every night for a week the nurse bundled Otto in woolen cloth, packed him in a cardboard box with cotton loosely stuffed around him to keep him from rolling about, and carried him with her on the one-hour subway ride to her apartment in Greenwich Village. Every morning she bundled him up and brought him back to the zoo, and the doctor noticed with interest and approval that Otto was gaining weight and size.

Then the doctor went away for five days of veterinary conferences out of town. And the nurse was on her own.

"Just keep things going the way they are and you'll be all right," the doctor told her before he left. "He seems to be adjusting to that formula all right. Stretch out the feedings in a day or two—once every four hours. Otto's getting to be a big boy now."

Things did go along all right for another day. Otto drank every drop of his milk and whimpered for more. When the nurse spaced the feedings farther apart, Otto was unhappy and so was the nurse. He clung to her fingers now, refusing to let go when the feeding was finished. He wanted more, *more!*

The nurse figured, reasonably enough, that Otto was growing fast and while he might have strength enough to go longer between feedings, he needed more food at each feeding. So she increased the supply from two dropperfuls to four. And still Otto cried for more. His furry little body stretched and swelled as he drank but, strangely, he appeared to be just about as hungry when the feeding was finished as he had been when it started.

"Otto, how *can* you drink so much!" the nurse asked him, when the noon feeding left him as round as an egg but still squirming and crying and reaching for the medicine dropper. "It's all right to be a growing boy—always hungry—but you'll *drown* if I give you any more! Now you go right to sleep, and in four hours you can have some more."

But Otto didn't want to sleep. He was hungry. He wanted more, *more!*

Despite the doctor's instructions, the nurse decided to go back to the three-hour feedings. The doctor certainly didn't want Otto to starve, and she noticed that when she changed the little animal's bedding, as she always had to do a few minutes after a feeding, that the liquid ran right through him.

The nurse also noticed that his body was surprisingly thin.

For another twenty-four hours she worked heroically to give Otto all he wanted to drink. She filled him up regularly every three hours; and, just as regularly, Otto's bedding had to be changed. And long before time for the next feeding he was stirring restlessly and giving his little whimpering cry, that meant he was hungry again.

The nurse grew thoughtful. She had had enough experience with human babies in her days of hospital training to know that formulas often had to be changed; sometimes they were too rich, sometimes not rich enough. Otto's formula had seemed just right when the doctor went away, and there had been no reason for him to order a change. But now . . .

With a good deal of doubt about the propriety of what she was doing, but with the certainty that the doctor was just as concerned as she was to rear this unusual baby, the nurse put in a long-distance telephone call to the university where the doctor was attending the conference.

The doctor wasn't there. With a whole party of veterinarians he was making a two-day tour of laboratories, and their schedule was so uncertain that the operator at the university was very doubtful if it would be possible to reach him.

Well, what to do now? A nurse who has been left in charge of baby animals does not casually interfere with the program set for her by her doctor, even when the doctor is not there to be consulted or at least told that an emergency has arisen. All through another feeding the nurse pondered what she ought to do, but when Otto drank frantically and seemed weaker at the end of the feeding than before, she made up her mind. She was going to change the formula, let the doctor say what he would.

It was easier to plan to change the formula than to do it. The nurse knew it was the Yale formula, but she had no idea how much to change the ingredients. Nor could she get any help from the reference books in the hospital library. The formula had actually been reported in a research paper that was buried among a dozen others on the doctor's desk; but, not knowing this, the nurse was completely in the dark as to how much she should enrich the mixture.

So she gathered up her courage again and made a telephone call to Yale University. After twenty minutes of being connected to one laboratory after another, she found a technician who knew all about the Yale monkey formula, and who (bless him!) complimented her on her guess that the original formula needed to be made richer.

"I sometimes get monkeys that need something richer," he said. "The formula works fine for nine out of ten, but now and then they do just as your baby's doing: they drink and drink, and it runs right through them. I just add ten per cent more evaporated milk and that generally does the trick."

Otto was, apparently, the first and only baby potto ever successfully reared in an American zoo. The nurse's diagnosis of what needed to be done to his formula undoubtedly kept him alive and started him off as a healthy youngster. When the doctor returned, the nurse carefully kept out of his office until he had dealt with the accumulated letters and papers on his desk, and then at the noon feeding she invited him to watch Otto having lunch. Otto had put on size and weight—

real, lasting weight—in the doctor's absence and was beginning to crawl and climb. Two fillings of the medicine dropper sufficed him and he willingly allowed himself to be tucked back into the cotton nest for his nap.

The doctor thought he was doing fine, and said so. And then the nurse told him what she had done.

"That," said the doctor, "is the best news I've had since I got back. You used your head. I should have figured that something like that might happen, and told you what to do. But you figured it out for yourself, and I'm proud of you!"

By the time Otto was three months old he was the pet of the entire hospital staff. Fat and furry, slow and gentle, he was the kind of baby animal that is inevitably petted and spoiled by everyone who comes near him. The nurse still attended to his feedings (they were on an eight-hour schedule now), and he was beginning to take fruit and tiny bits of meat; but it was Gus, one of the new hospital attendants, who devised the game that Otto loved so much. Gus noticed that Otto spent hours each day just climbing, up and down the forked tree branch in his hospital cage. That, of course, is not surprising, for pottos spend all their waking hours climbing through the trees in Africa in search of something to eat. But Gus thought Otto should have something more exciting to climb on, so he found a length of rubber hose. Otto would start at the bottom and climb eagerly hand over hand to the top, whereupon Gus would turn the hose upside down and just as eagerly Otto would start all over again.

"What we need is a machine to turn this hose upside down every few minutes," Gus said.

Not having time to invent or build such a machine, he fastened a hook on each end of the hose and hung it up in the diet kitchen, where he spent a good part of the morning. As soon as Otto reached the top, it took just a second to reverse the hose and hang it by the other end. And so Gus could get his work done—and Otto could have the time of his life!

Otto unfortunately grew up. And the mammal department, naturally, claimed him and put him on exhibition, so the zoo's visitors could enjoy his climbing antics. But on his record card in the Animal Hospital there is a detailed report of his birth and rearing, and the most careful notes about how to modify the Yale formula—just in case the zoo ever again has to rear a baby potto. And so Otto and his friend the nurse have made a real contribution to our knowledge of how to bring up a rare and delicate baby animal.

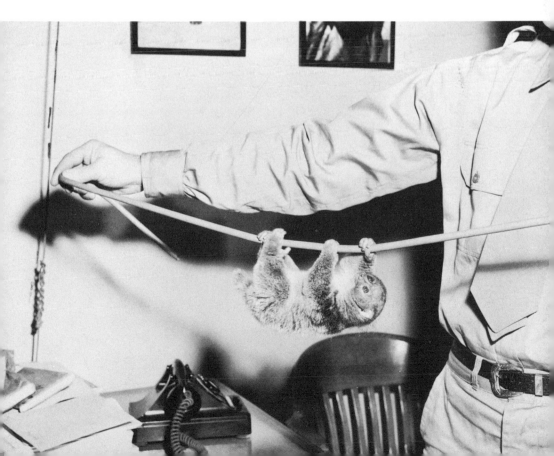

# Lions in the Living Room

Somebody once asked the zoo doctor if he could tell in a few words the difference between a zoo doctor and the kind of doctor who takes care of people.

He thought a long time.

"Animals get a lot of the diseases that people have," he said. "They get well if you give them the same kind of medicine. Animal surgery is no different from human surgery. Animals can't tell you what's the matter with them; that's one difference. But lots of times people don't know either; they can talk, and they often tell you about a set of symptoms that haven't anything to do with what's really the matter with them. Hmm. Let's see now. . . ."

He thought some more. "Well, doctors who take care of people don't take their patients home with them overnight and keep them in the bathtub—or in a box in the closet. And I've done those things with some of *my* patients!"

He was thinking of a baby hippopotamus and two baby lions, all born in the Bronx Zoo and all needing medical care.

When the pigmy hippopotamus was discovered, back in 1912, the Bronx Zoo was the first zoo in the United States to get some of those fat, black, oily-skinned curiosities from the jungles of Liberia. To everyone's delight they thrived in the zoo, and almost every year a baby was born. Usually its mother nursed it and took jealous care of it and the babies were no problem to the veterinarian or anyone else. In fact, the Bronx Zoo's collection of pigmy hippopotamuses increased steadily, the babies grew up and had babies of their own, and in a few years the zoo had to sell some of its surplus pigmy hippopotamuses to other zoos.

Then, late one afternoon, a baby was born and its mother decided she wasn't interested in it. She just looked at it a few minutes and walked away.

There isn't any good way of making a pigmy hippopotamus nurse her baby if she doesn't want to, and the doctor didn't waste time trying. The first few hours of the baby's life would be the critical ones, he knew; and he had to take over and do what the baby's mother should have done.

Warmth was the first necessity. The doctor found an old sweater in the hospital, wrapped the baby as snugly as he could, and put it on the front seat of his automobile. He drove home as fast as possible and filled the bathtub about a third full of warm water. All night long he sat beside the tub, massaging the baby, changing the water every now and then to keep it warm, and giving the baby a bottle of warm milk every two hours. And that was how he saved the baby's life.

The two lion cubs were a different kind of problem— easier in one way, but more trouble in another.

Sometimes zoo lionesses are not very good mothers. They get nervous when they have babies; the noise and excitement of the zoo visitors seem to bother them, even though they have a dark and secluded place where they can keep their cubs for the first few weeks. In the Bronx Zoo there is a small room just behind the big compartment where the lions are on exhibition. The cubs are usually born in this small room and stay there with their mother until they are old enough to wander out by themselves.

When Jennie the lioness had her first cubs, it upset her so much that she (like the pigmy hippopotamus) simply refused to have anything to do with them.

In those days the Bronx Zoo did not have an Animal Nursery, as it does now; and if the cubs were going to be kept warm and fed every three hours right around the clock, the doctor was going to have to do it.

Not only were they Jennie's first cubs; they were also the first lion cubs the zoo doctor had ever tried to raise. So he was just as nervous as Jennie was. Only Jennie, being an animal, couldn't be blamed if she let her cubs die; whereas the doctor was obliged to do his very best to keep them alive. And he was determined to do it.

His nurse was on vacation at the time, so the doctor decided to learn all about lion cubs by taking full charge of them himself.

He figured that a formula based on domestic cat's milk would be satisfactory for little lions, and feeding them was simple enough. On a table in the laboratory he spread out a soft towel, placed the babies on it, and offered one after another a bottle of warm milk. Each one seized the rubber nipple and began drinking with very little coaxing. It was almost too easy. The only trouble was that the doctor suddenly realized that the babies would have to be fed every three hours during the night—and that meant taking them home with him. And he wasn't too sure about what his wife would think if he brought home a couple of lions—even baby ones.

He needn't have worried. The cubs were certainly nothing to frighten anyone. They weighed just three pounds each, at first their eyes were tightly closed, and they were simply help-

less, sleepy little balls of fur. The doctor's wife liked them so
much that she insisted on doing the feeding that night; and
the next morning, when the doctor started to take them back
to the zoo, she begged to be allowed to keep them for a few
days. So the doctor made two little beds for them, in cardboard cartons lined with blankets, and fixed up a bedroom
for them in a closet.

It worked out wonderfully well. The doctor's wife had
never taken care of lion cubs before. But she had helped her
Irish terrier Gussie to raise a litter of pups, and she thought
that two lion cubs couldn't possibly be any more trouble than
Irish terrier puppies. And they weren't, really. They had to

be fed at regular intervals, but the rest of the time they slept or played gently with each other. They were actually less trouble than puppies, for puppies are always squirming and jumping and wanting to chew on something; and the little lions just wanted to sleep. Even while she was knitting, the doctor's wife sometimes held the cubs on her lap, although they often wound themselves up in the yarn.

Gussie was a big help after a week or two, when the babies' eyes were open and they were old enough to crawl on the floor. Gussie would stand over them, exactly as if they were some rather unusual puppies of her own; and the cubs soon learned that she was a friend. At first they growled at her and made tiny spitting noises, but nobody could be afraid of easygoing old Gussie very long. Soon they were willing to let her roll them over with her nose and paws, and when they were sleepy they would stumble around the living room until they found Gussie, and then lie down beside her.

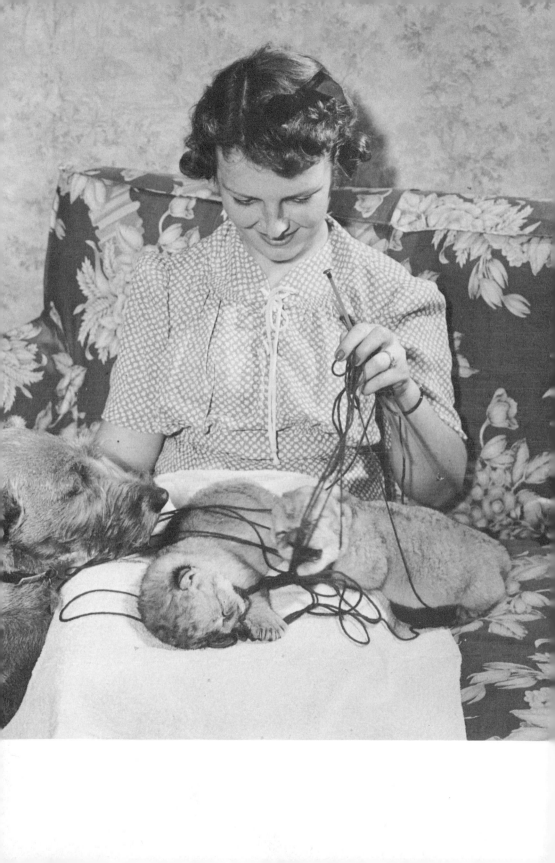

When the cubs were two months old they were almost as big as Gussie, and the curator of mammals at the zoo began asking the doctor when he was going to bring them back so they could be put on exhibition.

"Oh, one of these days when they get a bit more self-reliant," the doctor would say.

The fact was that the doctor's wife was having so much fun with the cubs that she didn't want him to take them back to the zoo.

But one afternoon one of her neighbors dropped in un-expectedly for a visit. Usually, when she knew visitors were coming, the doctor's wife locked the cubs in one of the bed-rooms; for they had developed a game of jumping out from behind a chair and chewing on people's ankles.

This afternoon both cubs happened to be just behind the door when the neighbor opened it. They jumped for her feet, and each one grabbed an ankle. They didn't really break the skin, or hurt her. But they ruined a pair of stockings, and the neighbor woman came pretty near having hysterics.

So the lion cubs went back to the zoo the next morning.

As the zoo doctor could have said: "The difference be-tween a zoo doctor and the other kind is that sometimes the zoo doctor's patients bite people on the ankle!"

# Bones Fixed While You Wait

Sometimes, when he was making his morning rounds of the animal buildings in the Bronx Zoo, the doctor stopped to talk to some of his animal friends. Very often he wanted to get close to them, to look at some little spot where they had perhaps worn off a bit of hair, or to examine their teeth or their hoofs. And he had found that if you moved slowly and talked in a low, gentle tone, even the shyest animals would sometimes let you get quite close.

This morning he gave a good lecture to Brownie, the young Arabian gazelle.

"I'm worried about you, Brownie. Your keeper says you simply won't eat your vegetables if they have vitamins and minerals on them. Don't you know that's a bad thing to do, Brownie? Don't you know your bones will get all soft, and one of these days you'll break a leg unless you take your cod-liver oil and your minerals?"

"That's a fact, Doc," the keeper said. He was standing beside the doctor while the doctor gently ran his hand along the gazelle's soft, silky coat of hair. "I mix his carrots and apples and cabbage and bread and stuff, just like you said, and then I pour the cod-liver oil and the bone meal over it and mix them in. But Brownie sniffs around and pushes the oily pieces out of the dish. He'll just eat the pieces that don't have any oil, or almost none. And if he doesn't get enough to eat in his own dish, he raids the other gazelles and takes the clean pieces from their dishes."

"Well, you can hardly blame him," the doctor said. "I wouldn't like my dinner all sloshed over with cod-liver oil and bone meal, either. But that isn't the point. Out in Arabia, where Brownie comes from, these little gazelles live in the bright sunshine and they don't need vitamins poured on their food; they get them out of the sunshine. But here in the zoo, in wintertime, they can't go out of doors, so they have to eat their vitamins. You keep trying to make Brownie eat his food properly; and if he simply won't do it, one of these days I'll take him to the hospital and see if we can coax him into doing it."

The doctor didn't know how soon Brownie was coming to the hospital.

Just a week later the keeper telephoned the doctor in the middle of the morning. "Brownie's broken his leg, Doc. At least, I think it's broken. He and one of the other gazelles were scrapping a little over their food, and Brownie slipped and fell. And he didn't get up; his left front leg's all doubled up under him."

"Well, I was afraid this would happen," the doctor said. "I'll be right over. Don't move him or frighten him."

The doctor gathered up a couple of blankets and made a comfortable bed in the back of the animal ambulance, and then he drove over to the Kangaroo House, where Brownie lived. Sure enough, the little gazelle seemed to have a broken leg; the doctor could see that at a glance, from the way it was doubled under the slim brown body.

"I won't scold you, Brownie, although I ought to say 'I told you so,'" the doctor said, as he entered the gazelle's compartment and gathered the little creature into his arms. "This is what comes of not eating your vitamins and minerals, just as I told you last week. Now you're going to have to have a cast on your leg, and you'll have to hobble around for several weeks. It won't hurt you, but it'll be uncomfortable; and you can't run and play with the other gazelles much before next spring. Now don't you wish you'd been a good gazelle?"

Brownie didn't say anything (not that the doctor expected him to talk back), but he struggled a little as the doctor carried him out to the ambulance and wrapped him in one of the blankets. This held his legs so closely against his body that he could not move; he lay quietly on the floor of the ambulance as the doctor drove slowly back to the hospital.

The nurse and the hospital attendant had heard the keeper talking to the doctor, and they knew an X-ray would be needed, so everything was in readiness when the ambulance arrived. Brownie may have been a little frightened when they carried him into a small room and put him on a hard, slick table with a thin, black X-ray film holder under his broken leg—and especially when the doctor pressed a button and the machinery at the end of the table made a buzzing sound for a moment—but he may have known that he was no longer able to leap up and run away. At any rate, he held quite still, and in a few minutes it was all over and the doctor had carried him into another room and placed him on a soft bed of hay.

"Take the X-ray film over to the photographic studio and ask them to develop it right away," the doctor said to the attendant. "If the X-ray shows his leg is broken, he'll feel a lot better just as soon as we get a splint on it."

In half an hour the X-ray had been developed and the

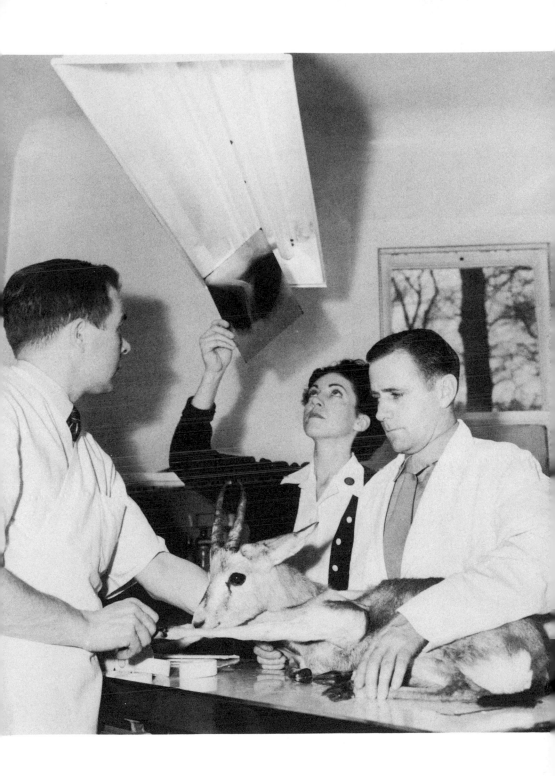

doctor carried Brownie into the operating room and placed him on another hard, slick table—this time a white operating table. Brownie's sensitive nose smelled all sorts of strange and frightening things; but his friend the doctor was with him and talked to him, and he soon found that there was nothing to be afraid of.

The nurse held up the X-ray plate.

"It's just what I thought—a long split, like a green stick," the doctor said, as he studied the X-ray of the broken leg. "Brownie wouldn't take his vitamins, so his bones got soft, and the least little push by the other gazelle was enough to make him snap his leg. All right, Brownie. We're going to put a splint on your leg and then you'll feel almost as good as new. Now this isn't going to hurt a bit, so just lie quietly."

And it didn't hurt, either, except for just an instant when the doctor lifted the broken leg. Then he placed light, slender

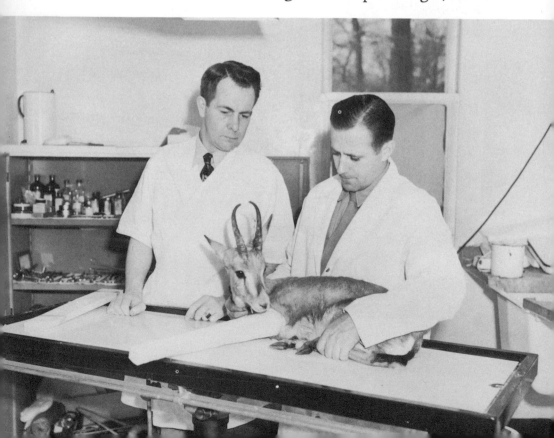

wooden splints on either side of the leg and bound them together with a roll of bandage, which he taped firmly in place. In a few minutes Brownie's leg was completely hidden under the bandages of the splint, and it stuck out stiffly across the table. It looked enormous—as if it were twice as long as his other legs—but actually it was just the same length, and the doctor knew that as soon as Brownie got used to walking stiff-legged on it, he would be able to hobble around perfectly well.

"Now I hope you've learned your lesson, Brownie," he said to the gazelle, as the hospital attendant prepared to pick Brownie up and carry him back to his bed of hay. "You're going to have to stay in the hospital for about a month, and we'll see that you learn to like your vitamins so this won't happen again."

The doctor made sure that Brownie had plenty of straw and plenty of room where he could walk around when he got used to the stiffness of the splint. Then he wrote out instructions for feeding the gazelle. Every piece of vegetable, no matter how small, had to be dipped in cod-liver oil and sprinkled with bone meal. Hereafter there would be no clean pieces that Brownie could pick out of the rest.

"He may refuse to eat anything for a day or two, but as soon as he gets really hungry and finds that he has to take the cod-liver oil in order to get anything to eat, he will," the doctor said.

He was right. By the next morning Brownie had learned how to stump around on his splinted leg, and in another twenty-four hours he was so hungry that he ate a few vegetables—cod-liver oil, bone meal, and all. And within a week he was taking his vitamins as regularly as if he had enjoyed them all his life.

"Brownie, you're just a spoiled baby," the doctor told him. "Look at all the trouble you caused me and yourself! Aren't you ashamed?"

Brownie wasn't ashamed at all. He just bent down and began eating cabbage and cod-liver oil.


On the afternoon of the day that Brownie broke his leg, the doctor had another patient with a broken leg. This time it was Paddy, the rare little Campbell's monkey from Africa. Paddy didn't break his leg because he wouldn't eat his vitamins; the doctor never had that kind of trouble with the monkeys in the zoo. Monkeys will eat oranges, bananas, grapes, carrots, lettuce, apples, raisins, peaches, bread, peanuts, celery, plums, and pretty nearly anything else they can get hold of. And they seldom care whether it is covered with cod-liver oil and bone meal or not; they just like to eat.

Paddy broke his leg because he slipped on a banana peel.

The doctor thought the keeper was joking when he carried Paddy into the hospital that afternoon and explained that the little monkey had slipped on a banana peel and fallen to the cement floor of his big, out-of-doors compartment at the Small Mammal House.

"Why, monkeys almost never slip and fall," the doctor said. "How did he really happen to fall?"

"Just the way I told you," the keeper said. "He slipped on a banana peel. It was this way. You know, I always give Paddy some fruit in the middle of the afternoon, and I generally give him half a banana, because he likes it so much.

I always peel the banana and I don't usually give him the peeling. But this afternoon one of the visitors saw me feeding Paddy, and I guess he thought Paddy didn't have enough. Anyway, before I could stop him, he pulled a whole banana out of a paper sack he was carrying, and tossed it in the cage. Paddy grabbed it right away, of course. He carried it up on that rock ledge in the back of his cage, and he peeled it and dropped the peelings right there on the rock.

"He ate the banana and then he jumped over to the wire at the front of the cage to beg for another banana, but when he saw me standing there looking at him I guess he knew he wasn't supposed to beg like that, so he jumped back to the rock.

"And he lit right on top of one of those banana peels, and slipped, and fell to the floor. And that's how he broke his leg."

"Well," said the doctor, "I have been working in the zoo for twenty years, but this is the first time I ever heard of a monkey's breaking his leg by slipping on a banana peel. Anyway, I guess Paddy feels pretty bad, so we'd better patch him up."

That wasn't as easy as the doctor thought it would be. Paddy didn't understand what had happened to his leg; he kept trying to stand up and jump, every time the keeper held him the least bit loosely. And of course he couldn't stand on one hind leg, and he started to fall each time he tried to jump. That made him very angry, and he screeched and chattered and tried to bite his keeper. Finally the doctor called the calm, slow-moving, patient hospital attendant and got him to hold Paddy's arms behind his back with one hand and grasp his long tail and his good leg in the other hand, so that he couldn't struggle or try to jump.

An X-ray photograph showed that Paddy's right hind leg was broken as sharply and cleanly as if it had been a stick.

It was a worse kind of break than Brownie's, for the ends of the broken bone rubbed against each other and hurt every time Paddy moved the least little bit. So the doctor decided to give him some ether and put him to sleep while he set the leg. Paddy wouldn't feel any pain, and when he woke up his leg would be in a splint and wouldn't hurt at all.

Giving ether to animals is just as simple as giving it to people when they need an operation. The doctor placed a little metal cone, like an upside-down ice-cream cone, over Paddy's face, and in the upper part of it he poured a few drops of sweet-smelling ether—and in a few minutes Paddy's eyes closed and he went to sleep. He was sleeping just as peacefully and quietly as if he were curled up in his own compartment in the Small Mammal House in the middle of the night.

Then the doctor went to work quickly and fitted the two ends of the bone together, placed splints made of soft, light wood on either side of the leg, and bound them together with layer after layer of bandage and tape. Paddy slept through the whole thing, and he was still asleep when the job was finished and the doctor told the attendant to carry him into the next room and make a bed of hay for him next to Brownie.

"He won't be able to walk or jump very well until his leg heals, because the splint is pretty long," the doctor said. "You'd better put him in the big cage with the shelf, so he

can sit on the shelf and stick his leg out in front; he'll be quite comfortable."

Paddy was still drowsy when the doctor went home that night. That was a good thing, because by the time he woke up there would be no more pain in his broken leg and he wouldn't feel bad at all. Before the doctor left, he made sure that Paddy was stretched out comfortably on a bed of hay and that there was plenty of food and water in the cage for him to eat and drink when he woke up during the night. The doctor turned on a dim electric light, so Paddy could see where he was.

"And the first thing in the morning, you look and see how Paddy is feeling," he said to the hospital attendant. "When you come to work, clean the hay out of the cage, and give him fresh water and some pieces of banana. He likes that. But be sure to take the peel off before you give it to him!"

The hospital attendant came to work an hour before the doctor arrived, and he found Paddy wide-awake and hungry. He had eaten all the food that had been left in his hospital cage and he was ready for breakfast. So the attendant fed him and cleaned the hay out of the cage, and Paddy hopped up on the ledge at the back and stuck his splinted leg out in front of him, just the way the doctor thought he would.

And that's the way the doctor found him sitting when he came to work.

Paddy almost looked proud of his big, important broken leg!

# A Quiet Morning in the Animal Hospital

If there was one job the zoo doctor disliked, it was writing what he called his term theme—a long, detailed report on all the things that had happened in the Animal Hospital during the past year. Every spring the doctor had to find time to sit down at his desk and read all the hundreds of record cards that had accumulated during the year. There was a card for every animal that had been treated for any kind of sickness or accident in the past twelve months, each one with neatly typed notes about the kind of illness, the kind of medicine that had been given the animal, how long it took to get well, and so on.

All kinds of things had happened in the course of a year. A tapir got pneumonia. A special box had to be invented to hold musk-oxen while their hoofs were being trimmed (as you know). An old griffon vulture developed a disease called bumblefoot and had to be treated with hot compresses. And these were only a few. The doctor couldn't possibly remember them all without the help of the notes he made while he was working on each case. So he had to read the notes, and then he had to write a long, long report that would be published along with reports by all the curators in the zoo.

This spring morning the doctor entered his office, groaning and complaining about having to write his term theme when he would much rather be going around the zoo seeing how his various animal patients were getting along.

The doctor's secretary, who never got a chance to walk

around the zoo and who had to sit at her desk all day and type up the notes that the doctor would study for his report, had no sympathy for him. "Now, Doctor," she said, "you know you've got to write this report, so why don't you sit right down, and I'll bring you the cards; and if you work really hard you can get it finished by noon. Then you can go out and play after lunch."

"Play! Do you call having to lance an abscess on a rhinoceros *play?* I'd like to trade jobs with you, young lady, just for this afternoon. Play indeed!"

Still grumbling, the doctor took the long file case of record cards that his secretary placed before him, drew out a pad of yellow paper, and began to take notes about the most interesting cases.

He read and wrote steadily for almost an hour. It really seemed as if this were going to be one of those mornings that almost never happened in the Animal Hospital—a morning when there were no emergency operations, no worried keepers coming in to report that an animal hadn't eaten the night before, no sudden call to jump in the animal ambulance and hurry off to some far corner of the Zoo where a baby animal had been born and needed the doctor's attention.

Then the telephone rang.

"It's the Small Mammal House," the secretary reported. "The keeper says the civet has fainted, or something, and would you please come right down."

"That's the best excuse I ever heard of for getting out of writing a term theme," said the doctor. "A civet *fainted?* What on earth does he mean? Civets don't faint."

"Well, the keeper thinks this one has, so you'd better go

down and prove to him he's wrong." The doctor's secretary laughed. "That is, if you didn't bribe him to call you just so you could get out of your office work."

The doctor picked up his little black bag of emergency medicines and hurried to the door. "I didn't bribe him," he said. "If I had, I'd have thought of a better excuse than that."

The animal ambulance carried him to the door of the Small Mammal House in a few minutes.

"Now, Joe, what's the matter? What's this about the civet fainting?"

"Well, not exactly fainting, Doctor, but she did kind of choke and fall over once, like fainting. It's that old civet we got from Africa in 1947. This morning I put in her meat, and she grabbed it and tried to swallow; but she couldn't. Seemed like she choked every time. Then she'd spit it out and try again, and once, before she got it out, she gasped hard and fell over, but I pulled the meat out of her mouth."

"What's she doing now?"

"She's on her feet, but something's choking her."

"Let's take a look."

The civet was persistent—no doubt about that. Watching her through the glass front of the compartment, the doctor saw her seize a small piece of meat and try to swallow it. Each time it seemed to stick in her throat, and out it came again.

"Hmm. How does she handle, Joe?"

"She's tough, Doctor. She never has tamed down."

"O.K. Get that black carrying case out of the back of the ambulance and get her in it. We'll take her over to the hospital."

When the keeper returned with the carrying case (a

roomy, lightweight but strong box with air holes in each end and a stout handle on top), the doctor opened it and stood beside the rear door of the compartment while the keeper drew on heavy gloves. Cautiously he slid back the door and then in one lightning-quick grasp he seized the civet and thrust her into the case before she realized what was happening.

The doctor snapped the lid shut. "Come on over to the hospital, Joe. We'll have to give her an anesthetic. Bring your gloves."

It took only a moment to load a hypodermic syringe with an anesthetic, and when the doctor was ready he gave Joe his instructions. "Get her out of the box and onto the operating table. You take care of her head and hind legs. Nurse, when he has her down, you hold the front legs steady. I'll give her an intravenous injection in the right front leg."

Joe opened the lid of the case and made an expert grab. The civet struggled for a moment and her breath came in deep, whistling gasps, but Joe kept a firm hand on head and hind legs and quickly the doctor felt for the radial vein and plunged the needle home.

"Hold on until she relaxes."

Gradually the taut body slackened and immediately the anesthetic took effect.

"All right. Now let's see what's the matter."

Obviously there was some obstruction in the civet's throat or mouth, and the doctor placed his left hand under her neck to lift her head for the examination. As he did so, something under the golden fur made him stop and explore swiftly with his fingers.

"What's going on here? You ever notice this, Joe?"

*Under* the fur, and under the skin, too, as the doctor saw when he parted the hairs, was something that felt like a hard, metallic ring.

Joe peered at the ridge under the skin and he, too, touched it. "I never saw that before, Doctor. But of course I haven't had any reason to pick her up before, and this time, with my heavy gloves . . ."

"No, it's not a thing you'd normally see. Seems to go all around her neck. Well, she'll be out for the better part of an hour, so we'd better get an X-ray."

The X-ray room was at the other end of the hospital corridor. Joe simply picked up the limp body in his arms and carried the civet to the X-ray table. The doctor cushioned her head and neck on the thin X-ray film holder, the machine made a whirring noise, and the plate was exposed.

Within thirty minutes the zoo's photographer walked into the hospital with the developed plate in his hand, still wet from its final washing. "I thought civets were wild animals, Doc. This one's got a collar around its neck like a pet."

"That's the trouble. This collar's under its skin. Feels like a wire." The doctor held the plate up to the light and stared at it. "And that's exactly what it is—a wire all around the poor beast's neck, and the ends twisted together under its throat. Probably put around its neck when some native caught it as a baby, and he never bothered to take it off. So it cut into the skin as the animal grew, and now it's all covered over. Well, that's easily fixed."

Back in the operating room the doctor shaved the hair from the civet's throat, scrubbed the area with alcohol, and with a scalpel made an inch-long shallow incision that laid bare the thin strand of steel wire. The nurse handed him a pair of shining pliers with a wire-cutting edge—an instrument which is seldom used in an operating room, but which comes in handy when animals get tangled up in wire fences. With a loud *snip* the pliers cut through the wire, and the doctor groped under the skin for one of the loose ends. A few tugs and out it came—the whole "necklace" of wire.

"If I had my way, the selling of that kind of wire would be forbidden in Africa," the doctor said. "I've heard about it from our animal collector. You can buy it in any native store out in the bush, and the natives use it to make snares for animals. It's cruel and deadly. Well, now we know why your civet couldn't eat, Joe. The hair won't cover up that shaved place for weeks, but she'll be all right."

It was still hardly later than the middle of the morning, and there was no reason on earth why the doctor shouldn't have gone back to his desk and the writing of his term theme. But there were so many things, now that he thought of it, that he ought to be doing out in the zoo. Yesterday the two tiger cubs got their first inoculation against cat enteritis. How were they getting along this morning? And that Père David deer fawn, born fully a month before the usual time—was it up and nursing today? The doctor knew very well that if there had been any trouble in the nursery or on the deer range, the keepers would have telephoned, but he was in a mood to seek any excuse for postponing the writing of that tiresome annual report. He headed the animal ambulance toward the north end of the zoo.

As he drove past the Elephant House he noticed that the workmen were setting out a new tree in the yard where the

elephants took their summertime exercise. This was the third tree the zoo had set out there in three years; every time they set one out, Sudana pushed it over. Now the maintenance men were trying again, and the doctor was glad they were getting it done, because the cleaning out of the hole for a new tree had left an unsightly pile of dirt in the yard all winter. The old dirt would be used to fill in around the new tree and what was left over would be hauled away.

The doctor watched the men working for a few minutes and then he drove away to inspect the deer ranges. The Père David deer fawn was trotting alongside its mother on its long, spindly legs. It seemed to be coming along all right; nothing to worry about there. At the Animal Nursery the tiger cubs were sound asleep after their midmorning bottle of milk. Their breathing was soft and regular. The cat-enteritis inoculations hadn't bothered them a bit. The doctor looked in at the Bird House. All quiet, except for the whistling, singing, and chattering of the birds.

The keeper of the Kangaroo House saved the doctor from having to go back to the hospital and settle down to his report for lack of anything else to do.

"Would you take a look at that giant anteater, Doc? She's off her feed again. It's that little cut place on her mouth that bothers her, I think."

The doctor nodded. "I wouldn't be surprised. I was afraid we'd have trouble when she got that cut place. But the trouble is, she's not really sick and I don't hanker to go in the cage with a healthy and active giant anteater."

"Oh, that's all right, Doc. Maggie wouldn't hurt a fly. If you want to examine her mouth, I'll just grab her by the tail and hold her up a little so she can't snag you with her claws."

"Think that'll work, do you?"

"Oh, sure. Nothing to it."

The doctor had long since learned that a good animal keeper knows how to manage his animals, and this was one of the oldest and most careful keepers. If he said he could keep Maggie from making a slashing attack with the long, curved claws on her front feet (the claws she had used in her native Brazil to rip open termite mounds almost as hard as rocks), he could certainly do it. So the doctor selected a bottle of antiseptic and a box of cotton swabs from his little black bag and prepared to treat the cut place on the giant anteater's tiny mouth at the end of her long and narrow **face.**

The giant anteater was hungry—no doubt about it. As the keeper unlocked the door of the compartment, Maggie roused from her sleep on a bed of hay and thrust out her long and sticky tongue, the way she always did when she woke up at mealtime.

"You'd think she hadn't had a bite to eat for a week," the keeper said. "I give her the regular mixture of milk and egg and chopped meat every morning, and she runs out her tongue and takes a few drinks, and then she quits. It's like her mouth hurts her."

"I expect it does. Now let's see you grab her so she doesn't grab me."

In one swift motion the keeper stepped behind Maggie, grabbed her bushy tail in both hands, and heaved her hind feet a few inches off the floor of the compartment. "That's it, Doc. See—she has to stand on her front feet and she can't reach up and swipe you."

"Keep on holding her a couple of minutes and I'll have this mouth fixed up."

The doctor knelt in front of the anteater and peered at the raw and inflamed spot on her mouth. Maggie had cut herself on a sharp piece of tin around the base of her compartment. She had broken the tin with her claws a few mornings before when she was aimlessly ripping at everything that would give her a chance for exercise. He dipped one of the swabs in the antiseptic and swiftly rubbed it across the cut place.

"This'll sting for just a few seconds, Maggie, but it'll do you good."

Maggie didn't know whether it would do her good, but she *did* know it stung—and when something stings you on the mouth, there is one thing you always do if you are a giant anteater. You slash out with your claws.

Maggie lunged forward, but she couldn't stand on her hind legs and slash outward, because the keeper was still holding her tail in the air. She rolled to one side and stood for a second balanced on her right front leg. That second was long enough for her to lift her left leg and strike.

The doctor saw what was coming and tumbled backward, but he was not quick enough. Maggie's claw caught in his trouser pocket and . . . *rrrrrip!* Keys, pocketknife, and a dozen nickels and dimes and quarters spilled, clinked, and rolled away.

"Doc! Did she get you?"

On his back on the floor of the cage, the doctor began to laugh. He knew that Maggie's claw had missed his leg by a fraction of an inch and the only thing damaged was his pocket and his dignity, so the horror-stricken look on the keeper's face struck him as funny. With one hand the keeper was dragging Maggie out of reach and with the other he was trying to reach the doctor's hand and pull him to his feet.

"Did she get you, Doc? She *can't* strike when I hold her tail up. She *can't!*"

The doctor scrambled to his feet and, with one eye on Maggie, now safely dragged to the far corner, began picking up his keys and knife and coins. Not only was his pocket ripped wide open; the claw had sheared halfway down the length of the trouser leg to the knee.

"She didn't get *me,* but I'll have to get a new pair of pants. Well! I guess we both learned something about giant ant-eaters, didn't we?"

"But, Doc, I always hold her by the tail and keep her hind feet off the ground when somebody has to go in here with her. And she never did this before. I'm awfully sorry. I wouldn't have had this happen for anything."

"Don't worry about it. No harm done—except to my pants, and I needed some new slacks anyway. This was a special occasion. Always before, when you held Maggie up, she wasn't in a bad temper; but this time the antiseptic made her mouth burn and she didn't like it. I should have figured on that and stayed farther away. It was my fault, so don't blame Maggie. Now, let's see. . . ."

Standing well out of reach, although he estimated that by now the antiseptic had ceased to burn and Maggie ought to be completely peaceable, the doctor peered at the tiny cut place. Yes, the antiseptic had covered it all over. Good! In another two days it should be almost healed, and Maggie could eat in comfort.

"She'll be all right," he said, when he and the keeper were outside the cage, and the gate was closed and padlocked. "She has plenty of energy and strength and if she only takes half her food for another day or two, that'll be plenty. I'll look in tomorrow to see how she's getting on."

"Doc, I never felt worse in my life. To think I almost let you get hurt!"

"Forget it! I'd go in there again with you and Maggie if I needed to. It's all in the morning's work—and now I guess I really have to sit down behind a desk and work on my report. I can't go around the zoo with one pant leg ripped open."

The only thing the doctor forgot was that the unexpected

is always happening in a zoo. For as he entered the Animal Hospital and put on the long white coat which he ordinarily used while working in the laboratory—and which successfully hid his ripped trouser leg—the doctor heard the front door slam and the shuffling of feet in the hall.

"Now what?" he said to his secretary. "If I'm going to get this report written by noon, I don't want any interruptions. See who's out there, will you? Unless it's animal business, I want to work right here until I finish this writing job."

His secretary slipped out, but in a moment she was back. "I'm afraid it's animal business. Rabbits."

Rabbits? The doctor knew the zoo had no rabbits on exhibition, except a few in the Children's Zoo—and they never gave any trouble.

"What'll we do with these, Doc?"

One of the workmen from the tree-planting job in the Elephant House yard was at the door of the office. He was carefully holding his cap upside down, like a basket. The doctor got up.

"You know that pile of dirt in the Elephant House yard? When we started to shovel it up to fill the hole around the new tree, we dug up a rabbit's nest. The old one ran away, but there were these four babies in the nest, and I'm afraid one of them got its leg hurt by a spade."

Four baby rabbits, probably a week old, were huddled together in the cap—too young to be afraid, their eyes bright and alert and their noses twitching to detect the strange odors in the hospital.

First a civet, then a giant anteater, and now rabbits! They were all unscheduled and unexpected; they had all interrupted his plans for the day. But not one of them could be put aside or neglected.

The doctor cupped his hands and picked the little family out of the cap. "O.K.," he said. "We'll take care of them. Just don't turn up any more, will you?"

"I guess we won't, Doc. All the dirt's shoveled back in the hole now. The nest was in the last of it."

Baby rabbits, no matter how they happen to come into the Animal Hospital, are just as much a part of the hospital's records as any other wild animal, and so the doctor told his secretary to make out hospital-accession cards for them. In the meantime, he had been examining the babies and he saw that the left hind leg of one little rabbit had been struck by a spade. It was bleeding just a little, and the tiny bones bent back and forth as the doctor's gentle fingers moved over the soft brown fur.

"Nurse!" he called. "Here's a splinting job. Set up the operating room, will you please?"

It was a simple fracture, the doctor saw, and could be repaired so easily and so painlessly that it would not be necessary to give the baby an anesthetic. He waved aside the can of ether the nurse was setting on the operating table and asked instead for the smallest splints, some tape, and some narrow bandages. Even the smallest splints, made of light, strong wood, were far too large for a week-old rabbit. So while the nurse held the four youngsters cupped in her hands, the doctor fumbled under his white gown and searched for his pocketknife. He had forgotten where he had put it after the giant anteater ripped the pocket where he usually kept it. When he found it, it took only a minute to split a splint,

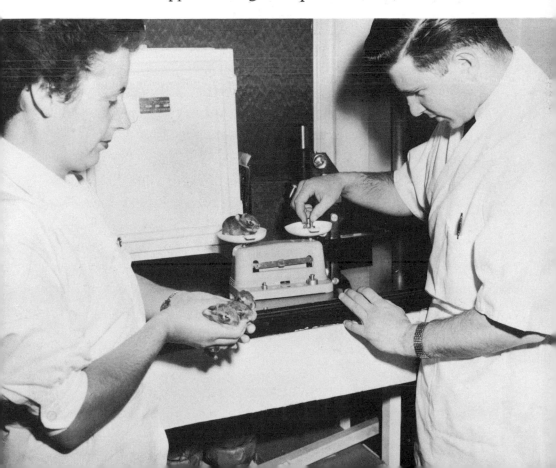

whittle it down to about an inch, and curve it so that it fitted the little leg.

The broken skin and the slight bleeding were not serious. The doctor washed the wound with a mild antiseptic, strong enough to clean the injury but not enough to hurt the baby, and then he wrapped the leg in a pad of cotton, fitted the splint, and taped it in place. Within five minutes the leg was bandaged, and although the rabbit moved a little awkwardly and had a tendency to hop in a circle instead of straight ahead (because it could not use its left leg), it was as good as new.

For the sake of the hospital records, the doctor had the nurse weigh each of the babies and enter their weights on their cards. They weighed almost exactly the same: 60, 61, 63, and 68 grams. The heaviest one, of course, was the one with the splint and the bandage, which increased its weight.

"It looks as if their mother's been taking good care of them," the doctor said. "I guess we'll have to do the same. I'm afraid you're going to have to pretend to be a mother rabbit, Nurse. Give them enough warm milk to fill about one medicine dropper every three hours for a couple of days, and then try them on lettuce. Little rabbits grow fast and you may have to feed them even oftener."

That was just the kind of job the nurse loved. She warmed some milk and settled down in the laboratory to give the babies their first feeding. And the doctor, at last, was free to go back to his desk and begin to work on his report again.

"Let's see." He grinned at his secretary. "You said I'd be through by noon, didn't you?"

Whatever the secretary said, the doctor didn't hear. For just then the noon whistle blew in the service yard just outside the Animal Hospital, and nobody could hear anything else.

"I sure picked a quiet morning to write my term theme," the doctor said. "I'm going to lunch before anything else happens."

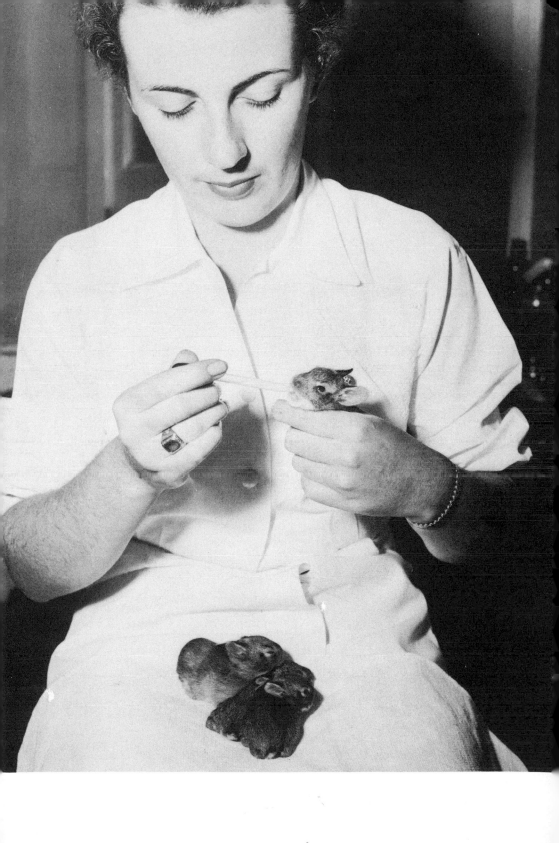

# A New Baby in the Zoo

For a long time there had been no babies in the zoo's Animal Hospital. Weeks and weeks went by, and although there were plenty of long-legged spotted fawns out on the deer ranges, and two baby monkeys in the Primate House, and several Canada geese waddling around the lawn and showing off their fuzzy, creamy-white goslings, all the mothers and fathers of the fawns and the monkeys and the goslings were taking perfect care of their babies and there was nothing the doctor had to do about them.

"What this place needs," he said one morning, as he came into the hospital after making his rounds of the zoo and seeing well-cared-for babies everywhere, "is a baby in the Animal Hospital so we can have some fun too."

The doctor's secretary was sitting at her desk and holding a telegram in her lap. She kept it hidden while the doctor went on talking.

"Do you remember the fun we had when little Kenneth, the wanderoo monkey, lived in the hospital?" he said. "And Otto the potto—what a time we had getting his formula fixed just right! Now nothing ever happens except sick elephants, or a tapir that needs an operation, or something like that. That's *work*. What I want is a baby animal we can have some *fun* with."

"Well, Doctor, what kind of a baby animal would you like? Maybe I can get one for you."

The doctor laughed. "I doubt if you could," he said. "You

haven't inherited a lot of money recently, have you? Because the kind of baby I'd really like to have here costs a good many thousands of dollars. You know that expedition we've got in Africa? Well, they've been trying for several weeks to get us a baby mountain gorilla. *That's* what I'd like to have!"

"No," said the secretary, "I haven't inherited a lot of money, but I think I can take care of the matter if a baby mountain gorilla is all you want. I thought you wanted something hard to get. Here, read this." She unfolded the cable and handed it to the doctor.

Arriving June 16 with cargo including year-old mountain gorilla named Sumaili pronounced Soo-mah-ee-lee badly spoiled darling insists on freshest possible vegetables.

"Hooray!" The doctor's whoop of joy was so loud that the nurse and the hospital attendant came running to see what was the matter.

"Nothing's the matter!" he called to them. "We're getting a mountain gorilla—that's all! One year old and badly spoiled already, it says in this telegram. Won't touch a thing except the finest, freshest vegetables! All right; we'll be ready. Nurse, your duty every morning is to go to the best vegetable store in the city and personally pick out the choicest lettuce, carrots, celery, bananas, apples, cherries, beets, and anything else that's in season, and bring back a sackful for little . . . what's its name. . . . ? little Soo-mah-ee-lee."

"So the poor little thing's spoiled, is it?" said the nurse. "Well, Doctor, I can see that's one thing you're not even going to try to cure!"

"Certainly not! Don't you know mountain gorillas are the rarest kind of gorilla, and this will be the only one in any zoo in the world? If little Sumaili wants fresh vegetables, we'll start a garden and raise vegetables ourselves if that's the only way to get them fresh enough. Nothing's too good for our Sumaili."

The nurse just grinned at him. "I've heard of grandfathers spoiling their grandchildren, but this is the first time I've seen a zoo doctor boasting about how he's going to spoil a baby gorilla," she said. "You're just looking for trouble when Sumaili grows up."

But for once the nurse was wrong. On June 16 the doctor was waiting impatiently at the New York International Airport for the huge freight plane that was bringing a cargo of wild animals from Africa to the Bronx Zoo. And when the plane taxied up to the freight ramp and the engines stopped and the cargo doors swung open, the doctor was the first person from the zoo to enter the freight compartment where a hundred kinds of monkeys and birds and pangolins and civets and porcupines—a whole flying ark of animals—were whistling and screeching and scratching and snuffling and making noises in their various ways.

"Where's Sumaili, and how is he?" the doctor asked the zoo's animal collector.

"Right over there in the big box, but it isn't a 'he'—it's a 'she.' And I must say I never saw a better-natured gorilla. She's spoiled because she's been petted and pampered, but on this trip back we couldn't carry the fresh things she likes, so she ate what we could give her—and some of it was pretty badly wilted and not fresh at all, but Sumaili ate it anyway."

It was dark in the far end of the plane, and the doctor turned his flashlight on the wide-slatted box. A shiny black nose and one bright black eye were all he could see. Gently he held out his hand, and a firm black hand reached out of the box and grasped his fingers. The pudgy fingers of the gorilla's hairy hand tugged tentatively, as if to find out whether this stranger was willing to play, and drew the doctor's hand inside the box. If she had jerked hard and fiercely, the doctor might well have been hesitant about letting a gorilla—even a baby—draw his hand in reach of her teeth; but he knew from Sumaili's cautious movements that she was merely curious about him. She held his fingers to her broad, soft, warm lips for a moment, and then the doctor stroked her face and felt of the coarse hair on her neck and back. It was clean and dry, and the skin under the hair felt soft and smooth—not lumpy with patches of dirt such as gorillas sometimes have.

"Sumaili, you and I are going to be great friends," he said. "So they couldn't give you fresh vegetables, eh? Well, just you wait till you get to the zoo. Your nurse bought you the best vegetables in all New York, this very morning."

Three trucks from the zoo were waiting to carry the planeload of animals to the zoo. Sumaili was loaded on the first one and, with the doctor riding beside the driver, it was soon on its way. Sumaili's new life was about to start.

"Jim, I want you to meet a good friend of mine—Sumaili. Sumaili, this is Jim. You must be tired after a trip from Africa and Jim's going to give you a bath, and then we'll give you something good to eat, and you can go to bed."

The doctor always liked to talk to his animal patients, especially the gorillas and the chimpanzees and the orangutans. He thought they felt safer when they heard a warm, friendly voice. And that was why he had taken care to introduce Sumaili to Jim, the hospital attendant, as soon as the truck arrived at the zoo and Sumaili was carried into the hospital.

"You know the routine, Jim," the doctor said. "Give her a good warm bath with plenty of soap. Then weigh her so we'll have a record of how much she weighed when she arrived, for I've got a notion we're going to fatten her up a good deal in the next few weeks. Then bring her into the surgery and I'll give her a thorough going over—although I would guess, from the way she looks and acts, that she hasn't got a thing wrong with her."

Jim cradled Sumaili in his arms, and the little gorilla put her arms around his neck and held on tight. She watched with curiosity and without a trace of fear while Jim half filled a sink with warm water. It was probably the first time in her life she had seen water flowing from a tap, and she reached out timidly to touch the crystal stream. The force of the water seemed to surprise her, and she drew her hand back and put her fingers in her mouth.

Slowly, so as not to frighten her, Jim lowered her into the water and then proceeded to squeeze water over her from a sponge. Sumaili enjoyed every minute of it. She dabbled her fingers in the water and once she smacked the water so hard with her hand that it splashed all over Jim. But he was used to that, and he just held her arms out of reach of the water while he gave her a good lathering with sweet-smelling soap.

Finally, when she was "clean enough to eat off of," as Jim told the nurse, he rinsed the soap off with more warm water and took her in his lap and rubbed her hairy body dry with a clean towel.

None of these things had ever happened to Sumaili before, but as the zoo's animal collector had said, she was a darling. Not once did she try to bite or throw a tantrum. Sumaili seemed to know that her new friends were not going to hurt her.

Weighing Sumaili was not as easy as giving her a bath, for it was important for her to sit very still on the bathroom scales and not rest any of her weight on the table where the scales were placed, or they would not register her true weight.

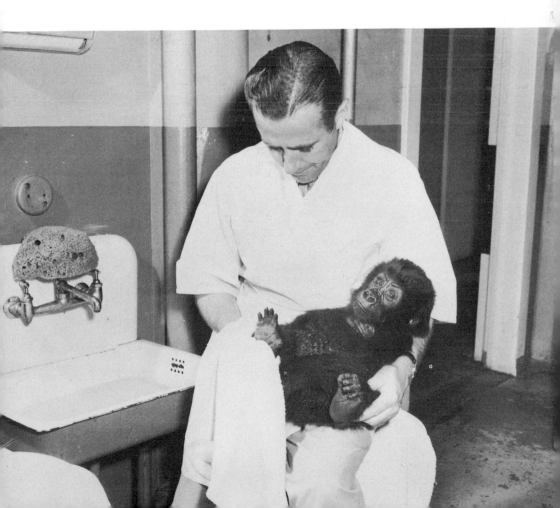

Sumaili's arms were so long that they just naturally rested on the table, but finally Jim solved the problem by putting a wide board on the scale and then covering it with a towel so it would be soft to sit on. After that, all he had to do was to keep Sumaili from playing with the scale and trying to make the dial stop turning by putting her fingers on it. But after a while she held still long enough for him to see how much she weighed. She weighed exactly sixteen pounds and eight ounces.

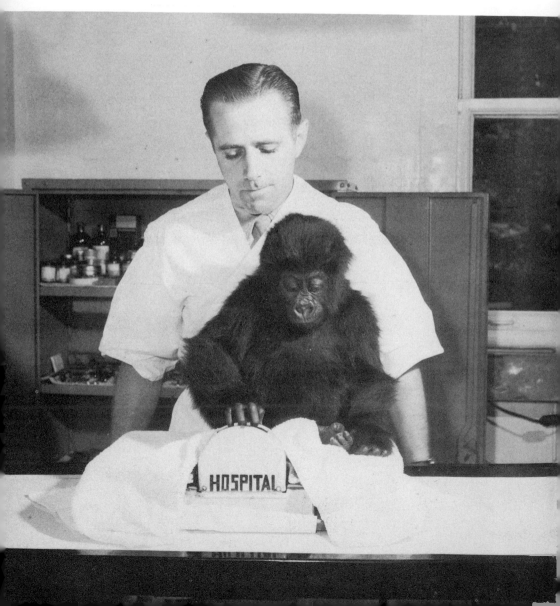

The only thing the doctor worried about was the physical examination he had to give Sumaili. He was afraid she would be frightened when he took her into the hospital's surgery— the small, white room where animals were taken when they had to have operations. But after her bath Jim took the little gorilla in his arms and kept talking to her as he carried her down the hall to the surgery. The nurse spread a towel on the long, cold, hard operating table, so it would be more comfortable, and Sumaili sat very quietly and watched everything the doctor did. There was nothing for the doctor to be worried about, for Sumaili held very still while the nurse put a thermometer under her arm to take her temperature, and while the doctor held her wrist to take her pulse. They were just the same things doctors do to people in a hospital, but lots of times babies and small children are a great deal more frightened than Sumaili was.

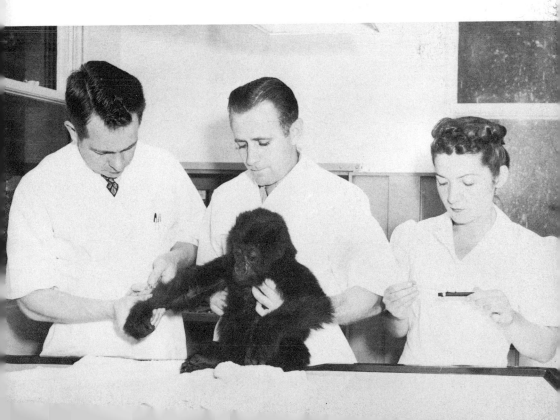

The doctor made all sorts of tests. He drew a tiny speck of blood from Sumaili's finger and looked at it under a microscope to see if she had any parasites in her blood. But she didn't. Her teeth were clean and white. Her hearing was perfect, for she seemed to like to hear the doctor's watch ticking. Everything about Sumaili was perfect.

The only thing that needed to be done was to find out what Sumaili liked to eat. That was the easiest of all, for the doctor had ordered a big tray of everything he could think of that a *very* particular little gorilla might like. There was rye bread, and apples, and beets, and bananas, and celery, and cherries, and cut-up pieces of oranges. He simply put the tray on his desk where Sumaili could reach it, and then Jim carried her in and let her sit on the desk. The doctor watched to see what Sumaili would choose first.

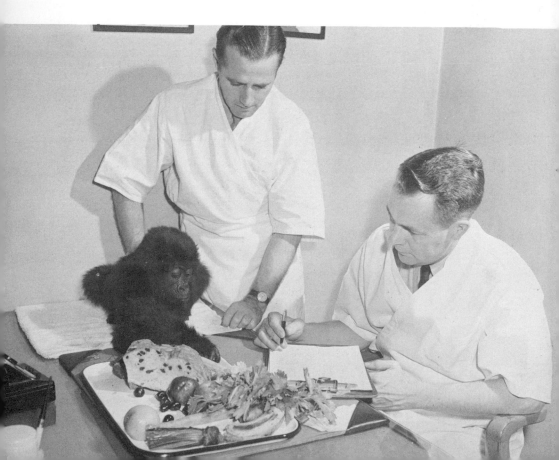

She began by touching nearly everything on the tray, and the doctor noticed that she picked up one of the apples and held it to her nose. But she didn't take a bite of it, because it was probably the first time she had ever seen or smelled an apple. The first thing she ate was a cherry. After that she took part of an orange, and then some celery, and finally she peeled a banana and ate a little piece off the end of it.

"That's enough for now," the doctor said. "I think I know what she likes. In fact, in a week she'll be eating everything we give her. She isn't nearly as hard to feed as they said she was. So give her a big supper and put her to bed."

Sumaili ate a few more cherries and finished the banana. Then Jim wrapped her in a thick little nightgown so she would be plenty warm during the night, and Sumaili was ready for bed. Another nurse spread a towel in the bottom

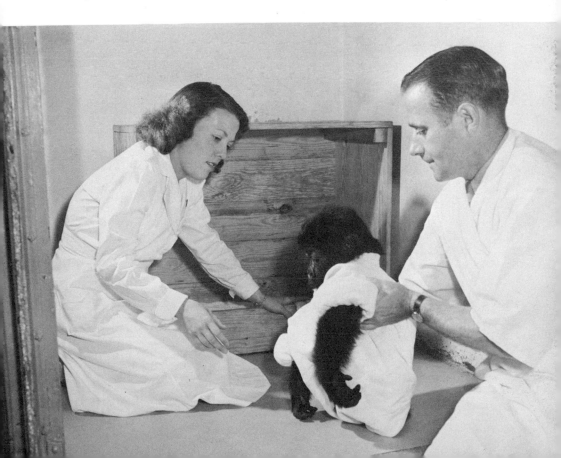

of the box that was to be Sumaili's bed while she was little, and even climbed into the hospital cage to show Sumaili that it was safe and a nice place to be.

Sumaili was very tired after her long journey from Africa. She pulled the nightgown close around her plump body and lay down on her stomach. But just before she went to sleep, she raised herself up on her elbows and took a long, careful look at her new friends, who were standing just outside her "bedroom" and watching her—the doctor, and Jim, and the two nurses. They smiled at her and said, "Good night, Sumaili," and Sumaili closed her eyes and lay down on her stomach again and went to sleep—her first sleep in the big zoo, among her friends.

And that's how the new baby came into the zoo family, and how the zoo doctor got his wish to have a baby in the hospital so he could have some fun!

WILLIAM BRIDGES was born in Indiana in 1901. After graduating from Franklin College, he went into journalism, spending several years as a reporter for American newspapers in France. In 1929 he joined the staff of the *New York Sun,* where one of his jobs was to write weekly stories about the animals in the Bronx Zoo. When the zoo's Curator of Mammals and Reptiles went to Trinidad and British Guiana in search of a rare tropical snake, Mr. Bridges was sent along by the *Sun* and wrote a series of articles for that paper about the expedition. In 1935 Mr. Bridges became Curator of Publications for the zoo, editing its magazine and technical journals. He has made a number of trips abroad, including two to Africa and one to Panama when he took along 10,000 live earthworms for three duck-billed platypuses on their way to the zoo. Mr. Bridges is the author of ten books, including *Zoo Babies, Zoo Expeditions,* and *Zoo Pets.* His home is in Pleasantville, New York.